"AMERICA'S BEST-SELLING TRUCK"

FORD
F-150
PICKUP
1997 - 2005

Robert Ackerson

"AMERICA'S BEST-SELLING TRUCK"

FORD F-150 PICKUP
1997 - 2005

Robert Ackerson

VELOCE PUBLISHING
THE PUBLISHER OF FINE AUTOMOTIVE BOOKS

Also from Veloce Publishing

SpeedPro Series
4-Cylinder Engine - How to Blueprint & Build a Short Block for High Performance by Des Hammill
Alfa Romeo Twin Cam Engines - How to Power Tune by Jim Kartalamakis
BMC 998cc A-Series Engine - How to Power Tune by Des Hammill
BMC/Rover 1275cc A-Series Engines - How to Power Tune by Des Hammill
Camshafts - How to Choose & Time them for Maximum Power by Des Hammill
Cylinder Heads - How to Build, Modify & Power Tune Updated & Revised Edition by Peter Burgess
Distributor-type Ignition Systems - How to Build & Power Tune by Des Hammill
Fast Road Car - How to Plan and Build New Edition by Daniel Stapleton
Ford SOHC 'Pinto' & Sierra Cosworth DOHC Engines - How to Power Tune Updated & Enlarged Edition by Des Hammill
Ford V8 - How to Power Tune Small Block Engines by Des Hammill
Harley-Davidson Evolution Engines - How to Build & Power Tune by Des Hammill
Holley Carburetors - How to Build & Power Tune by Des Hammill
Jaguar XK Engines - How to Power Tune by Des Hammill
MG Midget & Austin-Healey Sprite - How to Power Tune Updated Edition by Daniel Stapleton
MGB 4-Cylinder Engine - How to Power Tune by Peter Burgess
MGB - How to Give your MGB V8 Power Updated & Revised Edition by Roger Williams
MGB, MGC & MGB V8 - How to Improve by Roger Williams
Mini Engines - How to Power Tune on a Small Budget 2nd Edition by Des Hammill
Motorsport - Getting Started in by SS Collins
Rover V8 Engines - How to Power Tune by Des Hammill
Sportscar/Kitcar Suspension & Brakes - How to Build & Modify Enlarged & Updated 2nd Edition by Des Hammill
SU Carburettors - How to Build & Modify for High Performance by Des Hammill
Tiger Avon Sportscar - How to Build Your Own Updated & Revised 2nd Edition by Jim Dudley
TR2, 3 & TR4 - How to Improve by Roger Williams
TR5, 250 & TR6 - How to Improve by Roger Williams
V8 Engine - How to Build a Short Block for High Performance by Des Hammill
Volkswagen Beetle Suspension, Brakes & Chassis - How to Modify for High Performance by James Hale
Volkswagen Bus Suspension, Brakes & Chassis - How to Modify for High Performance by James Hale
Weber DCOE, & Dellorto DHLA Carburetors - How to Build & Power Tune 3rd Edition by Des Hammill

Those were the days ... Series
Austerity Motoring by Malcolm Bobbitt
Brighton National Speed Trials by Tony Gardiner
British Police Cars by Nick Walker
Crystal Palace by Sam Collins
Dune Buggy Phenomenon by James Hale
Motor Racing at Brands Hatch in the Seventies by Chas Parker
Motor Racing at Goodwood in the Sixties by Tony Gardiner
Three Wheelers by Malcolm Bobbitt

Enthusiast's Restoration Manual Series
Citroen 2CV, How to Restore by Lindsay Porter
Classic Car Body Work, How to Restore by Martin Thaddeus
Classic Cars, How to Paint by Martin Thaddeus
Triumph TR2/3/3A, How to Restore by Roger Williams
Triumph TR4/4A, How to Restore by Roger Williams
Triumph TR5/250 & 6, How to Restore by Roger Williams
Triumph TR7/8, How to Restore by Roger Williams
Volkswagen Beetle, How to Restore by Jim Tyler

Essential Buyer's Guide Series
Alfa GT Buyer's Guide by Keith Booker
E-Type Buyer's Guide
Porsche 928 Buyer's Guide by David Hemmings
VW Beetle Buyer's Guide by Richard Copping

Auto Graphics Series
Fiat & Abarth by Andrea & David Sparrow
Jaguar MkI by Andrea & David Sparrow
Lambretta LI by Andrea & David Sparrow

General
AC Two-litre Saloons & Buckland Sportscars by Leo Archibald
Alfa Romeo Berlinas (Saloons/Sedans) by John Tipler
Alfa Romeo Giulia Coupe GT & GTA by John Tipler
Anatomy of the Works Minis by Brian Moylan
Armstrong-Siddeley by Bill Smith
Autodrome by Sam Collins
Automotive A-Z, Lane's Dictionary of Automotive Terms by Keith Lane
Automotive Mascots by David Kay & Lynda Springate
Bentley Continental, Corniche and Azure by Martin Bennett
BMW 5-Series by Marc Cranswick
BMW Z-Cars by James Taylor
British 250cc Racing Motorcycles by Chris Pereira
British Cars, The Complete Catalogue of, 1895-1975 by Culshaw & Horrobin

Bugatti Type 40 by Barrie Price
Bugatti 46/50 Updated Edition by Barrie Price
Bugatti 57 2nd Edition by Barrie Price
Caravans, The Illustrated History 1919-1959 by Andrew Jenkinson
Caravans, The Illustrated History from 1960 by Andrew Jenkinson
Chrysler 300 - America's Most Powerful Car 2nd Edition by Robert Ackerson
Citroen DS by Malcolm Bobbitt
Cobra - The Real Thing! by Trevor Legate
Cortina - Ford's Bestseller by Graham Robson
Coventry Climax Racing Engines by Des Hammill
Daimler SP250 'Dart' by Brian Long
Datsun 240, 260 & 280Z by Brian Long
Dune Buggy Files by James Hale
Dune Buggy Handbook by James Hale
Fiat & Abarth 124 Spider & Coupé by John Tipler
Fiat & Abarth 500 & 600 2nd edition by Malcolm Bobbitt
Ford F100/F150 Pick-up 1948-1996 by Robert Ackerson
Ford F150 1997-2005 by Robert Ackerson
Ford GT40 by Trevor Legate
Ford Model Y by Sam Roberts
Funky Mopeds by Richard Skelton
Jaguar, The Rise of by Barrie Price
Jaguar XJ-S by Brian Long
Karmann-Ghia Coup & Convertible by Malcolm Bobbitt
Land Rover, The Half-Ton Military by Mark Cook
Lea-Francis Story, The by Barrie Price
Lexus Story, The by Brian Long
Lola - The Illustrated History (1957-1977) by John Starkey
Lola - All The Sports Racing & Single-Seater Racing Cars 1978-1997 by John Starkey
Lola T70 - The Racing History & Individual Chassis Record 3rd Edition by John Starkey
Lotus 49 by Michael Oliver
Mazda MX-5/Miata 1.6 Enthusiast's Workshop Manual by Rod Grainger & Pete Shoemark
Mazda MX-5/Miata 1.8 Enthusiast's Workshop Manual by Rod Grainger & Pete Shoemark
Mazda MX-5 (& Eunos Roadster) - The World's Favourite Sportscar by Brian Long
Mazda MX-5 Miata Roadster by Brian Long
MGA by John Price Williams
MGB & MGB GT - Expert Guide (Auto-Doc Series) by Roger Williams
Micro Caravans by Andrew Jenkinson
Mini Cooper - The Real Thing! by John Tipler
Mitsubishi Lancer Evo by Brian Long
Morgan Drivers Who's Who - 2nd International Edition by Dani Carew
Motorhomes, The Illustrated History by Andrew Jenkinson
Motor Racing Reflections by Anthony Carter
Motorsport in colour, 1950s by Martyn Wainwright
MR2 - Toyota's Mid-engined Sports Car by Brian Long
Nissan 300ZX & 350Z - The Z-Car Story by Brian Long
Pass the Driving Test
Pontiac Firebird by Marc Cranswick
Porsche Boxster by Brian Long
Porsche 356 by Brian Long
Porsche 911 Carrera by Tony Corlett
Porsche 911R, RS & RSR, 4th Edition by John Starkey
Porsche 911 - The Definitive History 1963-1971 by Brian Long
Porsche 911 - The Definitive History 1971-1977 by Brian Long
Porsche 911 - The Definitive History 1977-1987 by Brian Long
Porsche 911 - The Definitive History 1987-1997 by Brian Long
Porsche 911 - The Definitive History 1997 on by Brian Long
Porsche 914 & 914-6 by Brian Long
Porsche 924 by Brian Long
Porsche 944 by Brian Long
Rolls-Royce Silver Shadow/Bentley T Series Corniche & Camargue Revised & Enlarged Edition by Malcolm Bobbitt
Rolls-Royce Silver Spirit, Silver Spur & Bentley Mulsanne 2nd Edition by Malcolm Bobbitt
Rolls-Royce Silver Wraith, Dawn & Cloud/Bentley MkVI, R & S Series by Martyn Nutland
RX-7 - Mazda's Rotary Engine Sportscar (updated & revised new edition) by Brian Long
Singer Story: Cars, Commercial Vehicles, Bicycles & Motorcycles by Kevin Atkinson
Subaru Impreza by Brian Long
Taxi! The Story of the 'London' Taxicab by Malcolm Bobbitt
Triumph Motorcycles & the Meriden Factory by Hughie Hancox
Triumph Speed Twin & Thunderbird Bible by Harry Woolridge
Triumph Tiger Cub Bible by Mike Estall
Triumph Trophy Bible by Harry Woolridge
Triumph TR6 by William Kimberley
Turner's Triumphs, Edward Turner & his Triumph Motorcycles by Jeff Clew
Velocette Motorcycles - MSS to Thruxton Updated & Revised Edition by Rod Burris
Volkswagen Bus or Van to Camper, How to Convert by Lindsay Porter
Volkswagens of the World by Simon Glen
VW Beetle Cabriolet by Malcolm Bobbitt
VW Beetle - The Car of the 20th Century by Richard Copping
VW Bus, Camper, Van, Pickup by Malcolm Bobbitt
Works Rally Mechanic by Brian Moylan

First published in 2005 by Veloce Publishing Limited, 33 Trinity Street, Dorchester DT1 1TT, England. Fax 01305 268864/e-mail info@veloce.co.uk/web www.veloce.co.uk or www.velocebooks.com
ISBN 1-904788-86-6/UPC 36847-00386-9

© Robert Ackerson and Veloce Publishing 2005. All rights reserved. With the exception of quoting brief passages for the purpose of review, no part of this publication may be recorded, reproduced or transmitted in any means, including photocopying, without the written permission of Veloce Publishing Ltd. Throughout this book logos, model names and designations, etc, have been used for the purposes of identification, illustration and decoration. Such names are the property of the trademark holder as this is not an official publication.
Readers with ideas for automotive books, or books on other transport or related hobby subjects, are invited to write to the editorial director of Veloce Publishing at the above address.
British Library Cataloguing in Publication Data - A catalogue record for this book is available from the British Library. Typesetting, design and page make-up all by Veloce Publishing Ltd on Apple Mac.
Printed in India.

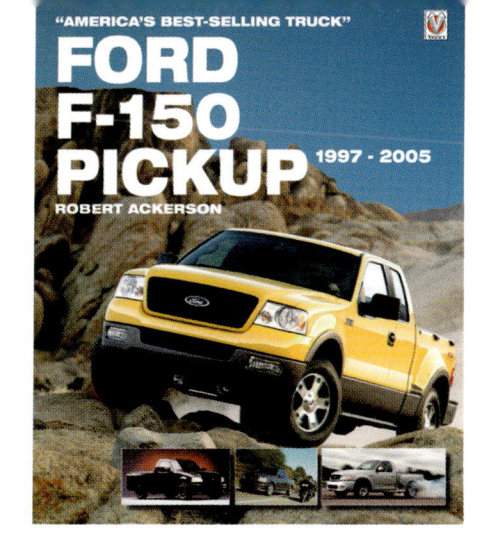

Contents

Introduction & thanks 6

Chapter 1 1997 7

Chapter 2 1998-2000 16

Chapter 3 2001-2003 51

Chapter 4 2004-2005 106

Index 139

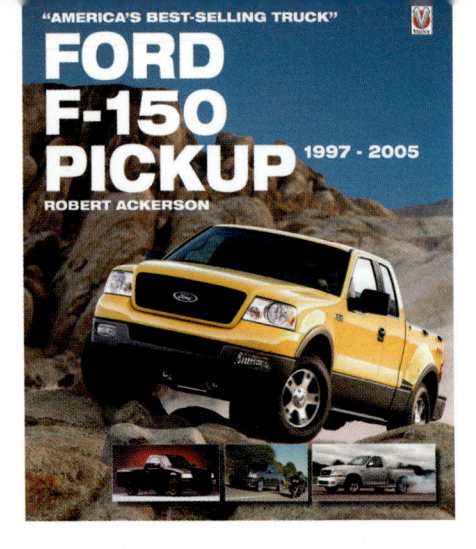

Introduction & thanks

The competitive nature of the full-size pickup market in the US is indicated by the scope of this book, the second volume of Veloce Publishing's history of the Ford F-100/F-150 pickup. It begins with the all new models for 1997 and concludes with a detailed examination of the next generation of F-150s introduced for 2004 and the subsequent models for 2005.

Ford celebrated the 50th anniversary of the F-series trucks on Jan 16, 1998, three years after the F-series had surpassed the VW Beetle as the bestselling nameplate in automotive history. In 2003, when it had been the bestselling vehicle in the US for two decades, it was recognized by automotive journalists as one of the 25 most significant vehicles ever built by Ford. Appropriately, this honor came as the Ford Motor Company celebrated its 100th Anniversary.

Like the Mustang, the essence of the F-150's enduring popularity is consistency. All the F-150 models presented in this book manifest a heritage of rugged design, contemporary styling, and the success of their creators in meeting, and often exceeding, the customer's needs and expectations in all aspects of modern pickup design.

The days when a customer needed to make just a few decisions when placing an order for a new Ford pickup have been relegated to history. Today there are dozens of choices of options, packages, trim levels, cab and box styles, engine/transmission combinations, interior and exterior colors, wheels and tires, radios, entertainment systems, communication devices, and navigation aids awaiting the truck buyer.

Moreover, owners can equip an F-150 truck for work or recreation, select a high performance model, or choose one associated with a favorite pastime or sport.

Let the good times roll!

Thanks

Special thanks go to the good people at Ford Media for making it possible to access the richness of Ford's great heritage via the Internet. But this system doesn't meet every need of the researcher and, for her help with specials requests, appreciation is extended to Marci Byrn of Ford Media Services. Thanks also go to Sharon McClellan of McClellan's Automotive History for her help in locating specific material about the F-150.

Robert Ackerson
Schenevus, New York

www.velocebooks.com/www.veloce.co.uk
All books in print • New books • Special offers • Newsletter

1
1997

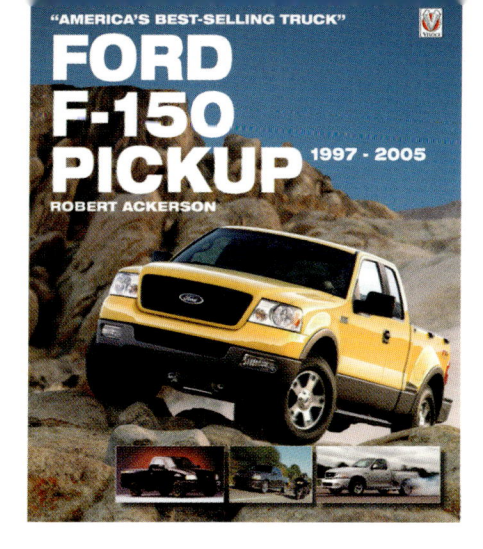

Ford's all-new F-150 combined its forebearer's toughness and rugged performance with an aggressive aerodynamic appearance and a host of customer-driven improvements in function, size, and safety.

Although designated a 1997 model, production of the new F-150 began in late 1995 with introduction occurring in January 1996. The 1997 F-150 was available in Regular Cab and SuperCab models in Standard, XL, XLT, and Lariat series, in either 4x2 or 4x4 configuration. The Flareside was sold in both cab styles and drivetrains in all series except Standard. Base interior was the XL trim.

Ford was debuting the new F-150 from a position of tremendous strength. With a 40 per cent share of the full-size pickup truck market in the US, the F-series had been the country's bestselling truck for 18 consecutive years. It had also been the country's bestselling vehicle - car or truck - for 13 years running. Extended cab sales had doubled since 1989, but capacity constraints had kept the market mix from exceeding 39 per cent. To alleviate this bottleneck, Ford scheduled the 1997 SuperCab to be built at all four F-150 plants in the US and Canada. Previously, a single plant had built SuperCabs.

Similarly, the 4x4 market across the industry had topped out at 40 per cent of full-size pickup sales because of capacity restraints. Ford's ability to produce 4x4s had been capped at 39 per cent because of capacity limitations. Ford hoped to improve upon this performance through production gains, as well as the appeal of the F-150's new off-road equipment package.

Chief program engineer of the new F-150, Tom Baughman, recalled that "when we sat down to develop the new F-series, we wanted it to be more than a successor to the current model. We wanted to take the whole concept of the full-size pickup truck to a new level".

The new F-150 still looked like a Ford truck but, with a modernistic front end and 56.7 degree windshield, wider stance, 16in tires (17in tires and wheels were available on 4x4 models), and a new bumper and grille format, its appearance was fresh, unique, and original.

The F-150 designers began by developing sketches of trucks that ranged from a sleek 'Revolutionary' model developed by Ford's California concept studio to an 'Evolutionary', more angular, traditional pickup. Positioned between these extremes were 'Muscular' and 'Personal Use' proposals.

Bob Akins, F-series chief designer, explained the theory behind this "bookends technique". "We didn't want to see six variations of the same theme. We wanted to see the total range of designs. We assumed that somewhere in between we would probably find an answer.

"The evolutionary design was not considered progressive enough", recalled Akins, "and the revolutionary design was too far-out. We needed to add some cues from the evolutionary concept to make the F-150 design more tough and rugged without losing what made it advanced - and that was the clean body side. The front-end ruggedness from the 'Muscular' theme became the winning design."

Acknowledging that the new

This 1997 Styleside 4x2 short wheelbase (138.5in) F-150 SuperCab was equipped with optional 6-spoke cast aluminum wheels and 255/70RX16SL OWL tires. (Author's collection)

F-150 retained certain characteristics of earlier models, Atkins added, "If you look at the shape of the grille on the 4x2 Regular Cab, this is a Ford shape. When the truck is coming at you, you immediately should know it's a Ford. That recognition isn't to be taken lightly. We saw the shape of the grille as an element to be retained."

The 1997 F-150's smoother front end and sharply-angled windshield, elimination of hard corners, and exposed drip rails improved aerodynamics from the 1996 model's drag coefficient of 0.48 to 0.45. In profile, the F-150's design was seen to integrate the cab and pickup box while maintaining clearance between the two to enable the box and cab to move independently. Other exterior features included horizontal pockets and vertical slots in the pickup box with tie-downs for added cargo capabilities; extended rocker panels for improved protection against stone pecking (wheel-lip moldings on 4x4 and Lariats were also provided for this protection); an integrated rear window halo molding with high-mounted stop/cargo light; color-impregnated rail molding to protect the box rail tops, and a locking tailgate.

"What we are doing", explained Dewey Holland, F-series marketing plans manager, "is redefining the look of toughness. It's not that square, boxy look. It's an aerodynamic look that allows you to keep your toughness. At the same time, you can be up-to-date ... In consumer clinics, we were shown again and again how the lines between function and family versatility blur as more buyers look for vehicles with multi-purpose capabilities."

Results from these focus group sessions were overwhelmingly positive, with high ratings given to the F-150's styling and more modern image. "We're updating the F-series with an equivalent leap forward in styling and features", Holland said. "In the same way Taurus took America by storm, we expect the new F-150 to become a benchmark to be emulated by competitors in the full-size pickup truck market."

To further strengthen the F-150 in the growing personal use market, Ford designers decided to diversify the line-up. For the first time the F-150 was available in models with their own identity. Again, Bob Atkins explains: "In everything we were trying to do, we were trying to expand a position of leadership, and it included diversity in models, diversity in the series of models, diversity in the powertrains, and even diversity in the range of colors.

"We went for the optimum of all the models instead of compromising them to make the 4x2 Regular Cab fit the desires and needs of all buyers."

An example of this philosophy was the 4x4 with its more aggressive grille front bumper with available integrated fog lamps and bumper tow hooks, and optional 17in wheels and tires.

The biggest design distinction was seen in the Flareside model. What Atkins depicted as "design stretch" was apparent in its new rear bumper, tailgate, and taillamps that wrapped around into the fender. "The Flareside", said Atkins, "takes us to a new height of personal use that should appeal to a younger market."

Beneath its outer beauty, the F-150 had an all-new chassis providing

The 1997 standard wheel for the Standard and XL models was this 5-lug Argent painted wheel with an Argent hub. (Author's collection)

The 1997 XLT had this Argent styled steel wheel with a chrome hub as standard equipment. It was available for the XL as part of a Preferred Equipment Package (PEP). (Author's collection)

This polished aluminum wheel was available as part of a PEP for the 1997 XLT. (Author's collection)

improved vehicle dynamics, ride, and handling. Using the comparable 1996 models as a benchmark, the overall length of the 1997 Regular Cab F-150 in short wheelbase form was 5.1 inches longer; that of the long-wheelbase version was extended by 7.5 inches. These changes increased seat-track travel and provided more behind-the-seat storage. Respective increases in the SuperCab models were 1.7 inches and 4.1 inches. SuperCabs thus had 23.4 inches of additional rear legroom and 2.8 inches more rear hiproom. All models had larger door openings.

Drivers and passengers alike appreciated the industry-first standard third door on the passenger side of the F-150 SuperCab. Inside, the SuperCab had more headroom, rear legroom, and cargo space behind the front seat.

The F-150's patented third door was a major design challenge. Rather than use a traditional hinge mounted on an additional pillar (which would have hindered access to the back seat), the F-150 design team opted for a hinge hidden in the cab's rear pillar. The system provides a 21in wide door that swings out 90 degrees.

The F-150 also offered numerous improvements in safety, including standard dual air bags with a standard passenger air bag deactivation switch. An optional, 4-wheel anti-lock braking system was also available. Horizontal and vertical door beams in the SuperCab's third door helped provide protection in certain side impacts and improved overall structural stability of the cab.

The interior of the F-150 was updated with a new instrument panel with easy-to-read gauges and controls, including larger radio buttons, positioned within comfortable range of the driver. The seats were of a new design and among the seat options were Captain's Chairs for the Regular Cab model. Other new features included cupholders that could accommodate large cups, a power point on the instrument panel for personal computers, phones or electric accessories, an optional driver's side secondary sun visor, adjustable safety

The 1997 Lariat had this 5-lug, 6-spoke cast aluminum wheel with a chrome hub as standard equipment. (Author's collection).

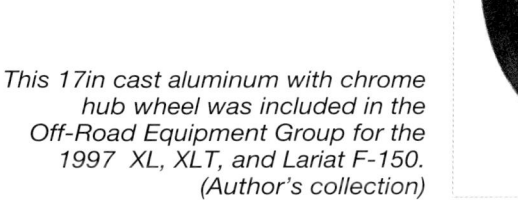

This 17in cast aluminum with chrome hub wheel was included in the Off-Road Equipment Group for the 1997 XL, XLT, and Lariat F-150. (Author's collection)

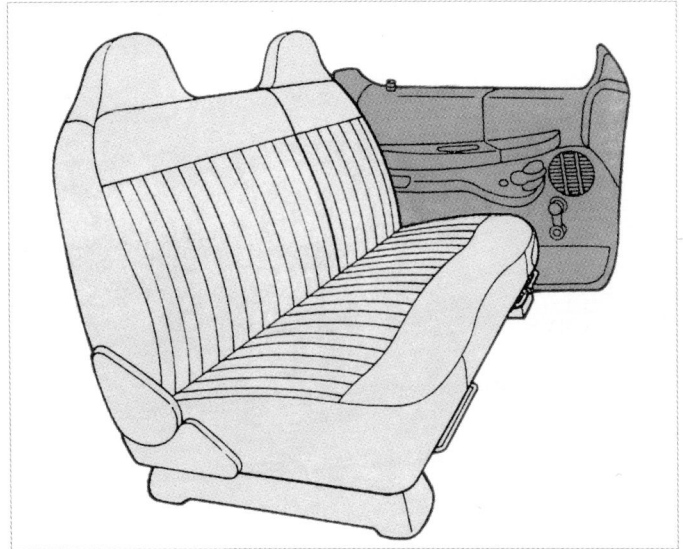

Left: The base split-back bench seat for the Standard and XL F-150s. The Standard seat was vinyl covered. The XL seat had a 3 cloth, poly-knit finish. The Standard seats were available in Medium Graphite or Medium Prairie Tan. In addition to those colors the XL seat was available in Cordovan or Willow Green. (Author's collection)

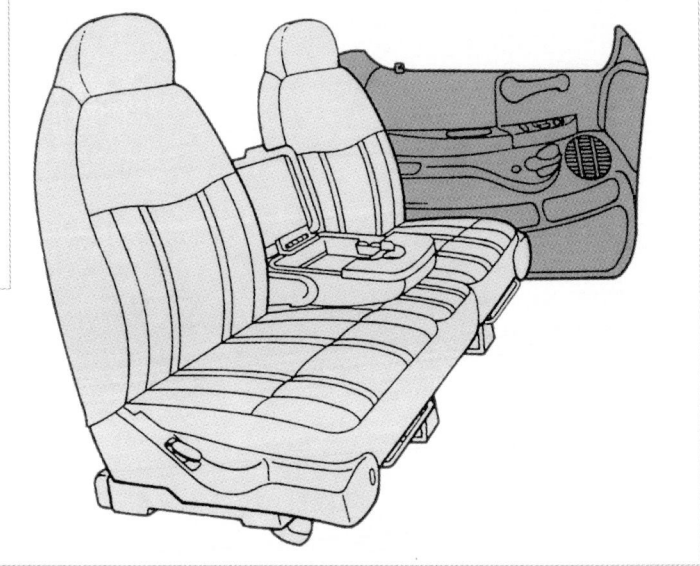

belts in outboard front seat positions (except for SuperCab's passenger side), and a standard acoustic cloth headliner. New convenience options included illuminated power window switches on the door armrest and illuminated speed control switches on the steering wheel.

The F-150 had the most powerful standard powertrain in its class; a new 4.2 liter, 90 degree V-6. Two technologically advanced Triton V-8 engines were optional. A 4.6 liter was available initially, with a larger 5.4 liter version added in the fall of 1996. All three engines provided improved fuel economy and could be coupled with either a 5-speed manual or 4-speed electronically controlled automatic transmission. All engines had stainless steel exhaust systems that exited in front of the right rear tire. This had two benefits: torque and horsepower output was increased because of the shorter path of the exhaust system, and the likelihood of damage to the tailpipe was reduced.

Derived from Ford's existing 3.8 liter V-6 Essex engine, the 4.2 liter engine was the most powerful standard V-6 in a full-size pickup with 210 horsepower at 5000rpm and 255lb/ft of torque at 3000rpm. Among its features was an aluminum high-flow split intake port, two-valve cylinder head design with swirl port technology, and sand-cast exhaust ports for improved air flow.

The Triton V-8 was the first of Ford's new family of modular truck engines. With 210 horsepower at 4400rpm and 290lb/ft of torque at 3250rpm, the Triton endowed the F-150 with the highest payload of any full-size pickup - 2435 pounds. Advanced sealing technology provided the Triton with durability and protection from potential damage caused by dirt and dust. The basic architecture of the Triton V-8 included a chain-driven single overhead cam, a deep-skirted cylinder block, cross-bolted bearing caps, deep-mounted cylinder head bolts, specially coated all-aluminum pistons, and three-layer steel head gaskets.

A 'Failsafe' cooling system helped protect the engine against damage from overheating, while allowing the truck to be driven temporarily before component damage was incurred.

Standard transmission for both engines was Ford's 5-speed M5R2, which was also used in the 1996 F150. The 1996 F-150 optional 4R70W fully electronic 4-speed automatic, with lockup torque converter, was available for the 1997 F-150.

All engines had platinum-tipped sparkplugs with recommended tune up intervals of 100,000 miles under normal driving conditions with routine fluid and filter changes. A six quart oil capacity was provided.

Use of larger standard wheels permitted installation of front brakes with larger rotors and pads and dual-piston calipers.

The F-150's all-new front suspension consisted of twin-forged short and long arms (SLA) with forged steel upper control arms. This design allowed engineers to eliminate the swing axles under the engine that had been an integral part of the Twin-I-Beam design, which made a lower hood line possible. 4-wheel drive models had cast lower arms, cast spindle, forged steel upper arms, an anti-sway bar, and torsion bars instead of coil springs. The optional off-road package included selected spring rates, heavy-duty shock absorbers, and component shielding.

Opposite below: The XL 1 40/60 cloth bench seat included recliners, armrest and a driver's side manual lumbar support. Its color selection was the same as the XL's. (Author's collection)

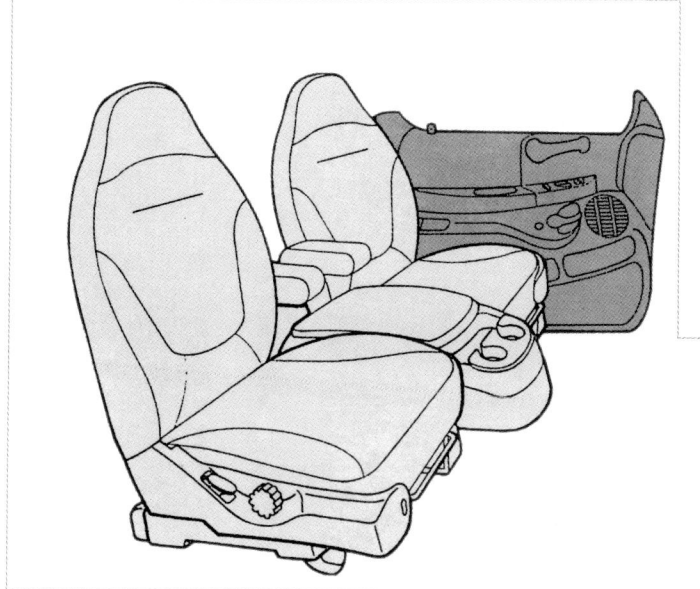

The Lariat's standard split bench seat with leather seating areas. It included recliners, armrest and driver's side lumbar support. (Author's collection)

The cloth Captain's Chairs and console option for the XLT. The driver's seat had a manual lumbar support. It was available in all four trim colors. (Author's collection)

At the rear, the 4x2 model used a Hotchkiss suspension, with a solid axle and leaf springs. The 4x4 rear suspension featured a solid Hotchkiss axle, with direct-acting 1 3/16 inch shock absorbers. Larger 1 3/8 inch shock absorbers were optional.

Summing up the quality of the 4x2 suspension system, Bob Westphal, F-series chassis manager, reported that "we've done an outstanding job of improving the truck's on-the-road feel ... And the truck's tough. We kept the traditional toughness in the truck's suspension, because that's what people want. And we made everything stronger, tougher, better.

"In the 4x4 front suspension, the torsion bar on the lower arm enabled us to more readily package the driving mechanism of a front-drive axle and still retain the low height of our powertrain.

"It has given us a very stable vehicle for off-road use and very good traction for the front axle, with very little bounce out of the front end."

Validating the F-150's "Ford Tough" label was a program of more than five million miles of durability, development, and evaluation testing. "We looked at the entire F-150 truck, component by component, sub-system by sub-system", explained Bob Himes, Ford's vehicle engineering manager. "Using our field experience, plus durability and other testing procedures, we did what was necessary to make the truck Ford Tough."

The site of much of the road testing of the F-150 was Ford's Arizona Proving Ground in Yucca, Arizona. Powertrains, cooling systems, front end systems, electrical systems, and anti-corrosion elements were tested on fifty miles of specialty roads, including grades of 20 and 30 per cent, and a series of torturous exercises.

Three factors dominated the F-150 testing. "First", recalled Bob Himes, "we designed all of these systems from a standpoint of durability. Next, we toughened our cooling temperature specifications for the best possible life. Then came the prove-out testing to verify that our expectations matched results."

The F-150's powertrains, front and rear suspensions, body and frame structure, and cooling and accessory systems were subjected to over 71,000 miles of Arizona Proving Ground durability testing. The Arizona area provided a unique combination of climate and topography - from 500 to 3900 feet above sea level and an average maximum summer temperature of 103 degrees Fahrenheit with peak temperatures of 120 degrees Fahrenheit.

The standards established for the 1997 F-150 were heightened considerably over already stringent durability levels. For example, supplemental powertrain durability testing added 22,700 miles and thousands of additional stops and starts to the cycle.

The Proving Ground's fifty miles of specialty roads were used for a series of tests known as the Sandwash, Twist Ditch, Translator Hill, Power Hop Hill, and Mudbath.

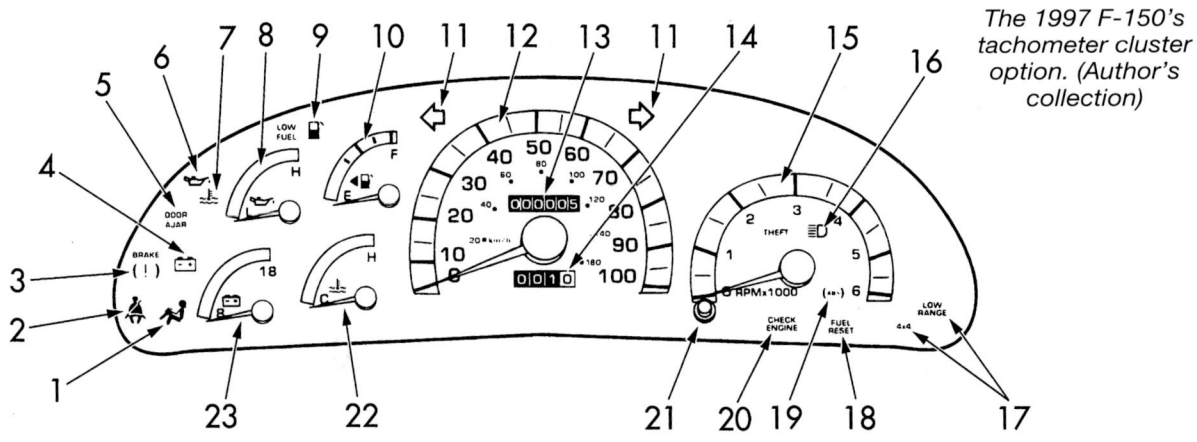

The 1997 F-150's tachometer cluster option. (Author's collection)

1. Air bag readiness indicator/warning light
2. Fasten safety belt warning light
3. Brake system warning light/parking brake indicator
4. Charging system warning light
5. Door ajar warning light
6. Oil pressure warning light
7. Engine coolant temperature warning light
8. Engine oil pressure gauge
9. Low fuel warning light
10. Fuel gauge
11. Turn signal indicators
12. Speedometer
13. Odometer
14. Trip odometer
15. Tachometer
16. High-beam indicator
17. 4x4 indicator light*
18. Fuel pump inertia shutoff switch indicator
19. Anti-Lock Braking System warning light
20. Check engine warning light (see Owner Guide)
21. Trip odometer reset button
22. Engine coolant temperature gauge
23. Voltmeter gauge

* If equipped.

In essence, the Sandwash was a giant sandbox. Only 4-wheel drive vehicles could successfully traverse its two-feet-deep sand. Each 1997 F-150 4x4 prototype completed 882 miles in the Sandwash area.

The Twist Ditch tested 4x4 frame and body durability on an F-150 driven diagonally through a large ditch. When the F-150 was in the ditch, its weight was largely supported on diagonally-opposite wheels, inducing maximum torsional loading of the body and frame structure. Each 4x4 test vehicle was driven through the ditch 3465 times. There was no pickup-box-to-cab contact or sheet metal damage.

The Translator Hill, a 3900 foot peak located in the Hulalapi Mountains, with a boulder-strewn surface, tested the F-150 4x4's gradabilty, braking, and powertrain durability. Each 4x4 prototype completed 105 miles on Translator Hill.

Power Hop Hill, a man-made hill with a washboard driving surface, was designed to test impact resistance and strength of suspension and driveline components. Each 4x2 F-150 prototype was driven without incidence through 288 cycles of Power Hop Hill.

The Mudbath was a concrete-lined enclosure filled with a mixture of mud and clay which clung to every part of a truck it touched. The purpose of the Mudbath was to test the retention of wiring and mudpacking resistance of rotating components. Each F-150 4x4 prototype plowed through 210 cycles of the Mudbath.

Clearly, the latest F-150 - with its combination of durability and handsome functionality - was a truck that would have made both Henry and Edsel Ford very proud.

Initially, the F-150's selection of exterior Clearcoat Metallic colors consisted of Light Saddle Tan, Bright Red, Dark Toreador Red, Moonlight Blue, Pacific Green, Teal, Black, Portolino Blue, and Oxford White. In the fall, Light Saddle Tan was replaced by Light Prairie Tan Clearcoat Metallic. Coinciding with this change was the deletion of the Medium Mocha interior color and the availability of a Medium Prairie Tan color. Remaining available were Cordovan, Willow Green, and Medium Graphite.

During the model run, the Regular Cab's rear storage pocket was replaced by a rear storage tray. This change did not take place if the F-150 was equipped with a CD changer. Both leather Captain's Chairs, with console for the Lariat, and carpeted floor mats for the XLT (including rear mats on SuperCabs), were "Delayed Availability" options for the 1997 F-150.

In 1997 the F-series was voted "North American Truck of the Year" by a panel of 47 auto writers and "Truck of the Year" by *Motor Trend* magazine. An extended model year enabled Ford to sell one million F-series trucks. In addition, the F-series outsold 38 of the 43 automotive franchises doing business in North America. It also outsold the two bestselling cars in America combined.

Details of the standard F-150 instrument cluster. (Author's collection)

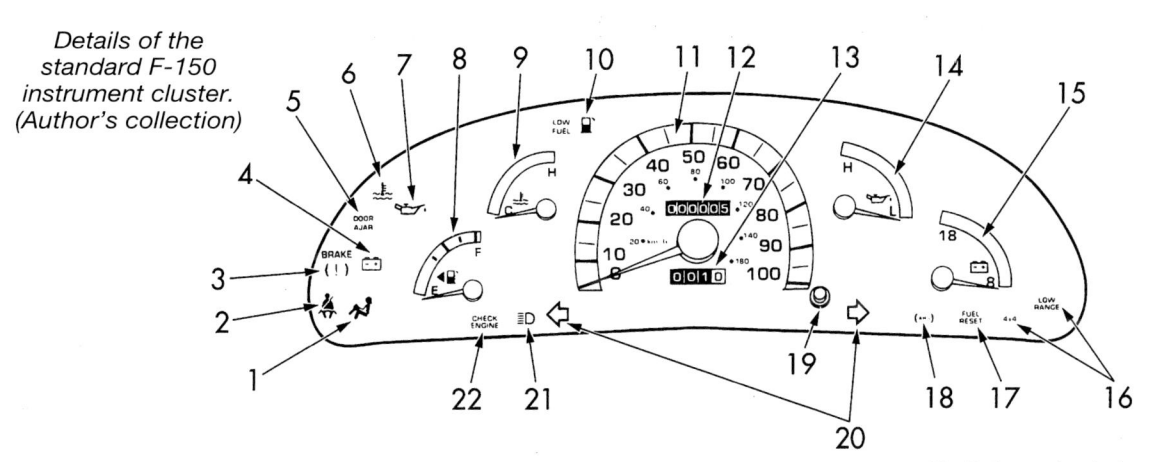

1. Air bag readiness indicator/warning light
2. Fasten safety belt warning light
3. Brake system warning light/parking brake indicator
4. Charging system warning light
5. Door ajar warning light
6. Engine coolant temperature warning light
7. Oil pressure warning light
8. Fuel gauge
9. Engine coolant temperature gauge
10. Low fuel warning light
11. Speedometer
12. Odometer
13. Trip odometer
14. Engine oil pressure gauge
15. Voltmeter gauge
16. 4x4 indicator lights*
17. Fuel pump inertia shutoff switch indicator
18. Anti-lock Braking System warning light
19. Trip odometer reset button
20. Turn signal indicators
21. High-beam indicator
22. Check engine warning light (see Owner Guide)

* If equipped.

Identification of the content of the standard F-150 instrument panel. (Author's collection)

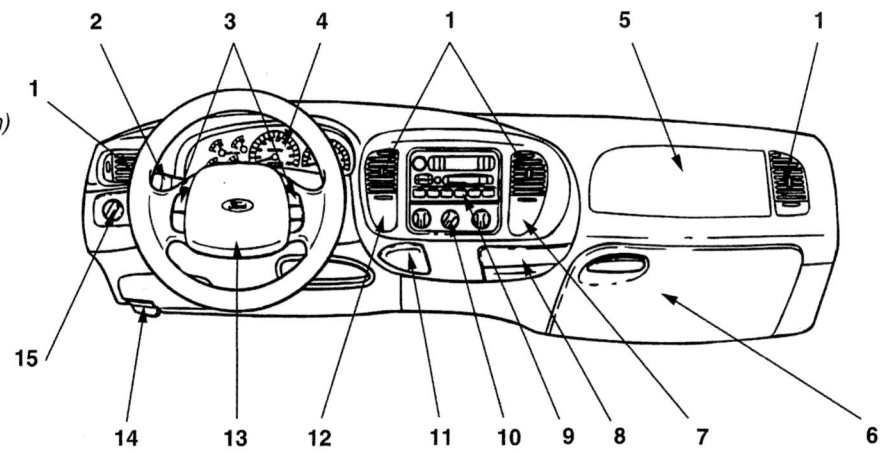

1. Air registers
2. Multi-function switch lever
3. Speed control switches
4. Instrument cluster
5. Front Passenger Air Bag SRS
6. Glove compartment
7. Passenger air bag deactivation switch location
8. Cup holder
9. Audio system controls
10. Climate controls
11. Cigarette lighter and 12-volt power point receptacle
12. 4x4 switch location*
13. Driver Air Bag SRS
14. Hood release
15. Headlamp switch

* If equipped.

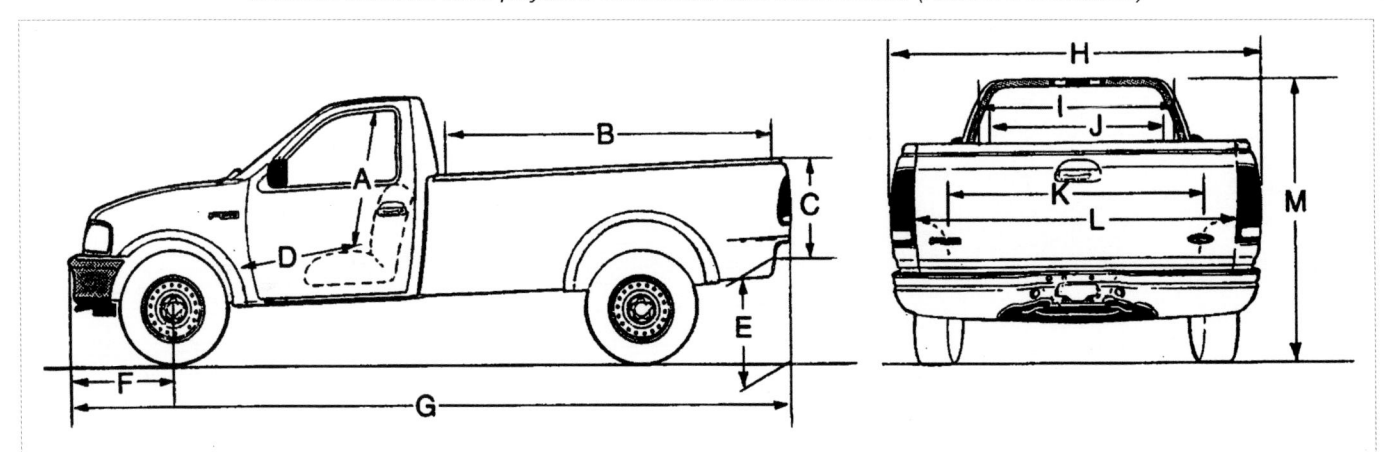

Both pages: These comparisons of the F-150 Regular Cab and SuperCab models and their Styleside and Flareside versions indicate their physical similarities and differences. (Author's collection)

F-150/F-250 Regular Cab

Model		F-150 Styleside				F-150 Flareside		F-250 Styleside	
Drive		4x2		4x4		4x2	4x4	4x2	4x4
Wheelbase (in.)		119.9	138.5	120.2	138.8	119.9	120.2	138.5	138.8
Code	Description	Inches	Inches	Inches	Inches	Inches	Inches	Inches	Inches
A	Head Room	40.8	40.8	40.8	40.8	40.8	40.8	40.8	40.8
B	Inside Length[1]	78.8	97.0	78.8	97.0	78.8	78.8	97.0	97.0
C	Inside Height[1]	20.0	20.0	20.0	20.0	20.0	20.0	20.0	20.0
D	Leg Room	40.9	40.9	40.9	40.9	40.9	40.9	40.9	40.9
E	Load Height (Empty)[2]	32.5	32.3	35.0	34.9	32.5	35.0	33.0	36.6
	Load Height (Loaded)[2]	26.6	26.4	29.5	29.7	26.5	29.5	27.1	30.7
F	Front Overhang	37.2	37.2	38.7	38.7	37.2	38.7	37.2	38.7
G	Overall Length[3]	202.2	220.8	203.7	222.3	205.9	207.4	220.8	222.3
H	Width (Max.)	78.4	78.4	79.5	79.5	79.1	79.5	78.4	79.5
I	Shoulder Room	63.8	63.8	63.8	63.8	63.8	63.8	63.8	63.8
J	Hip Room	61.3	61.3	61.3	61.3	61.3	61.3	61.3	61.3
K	Width Between Wheelhouses[1]	50.0	50.0	50.0	50.0	50.0	50.0	50.0	50.0
L	Load Width (Max.)[1]	65.2	65.2	65.2	65.2	59.7	59.7	65.2	65.2
M	Cab Height (Empty)[2]	72.7	72.4	75.4	75.1	72.7	75.4	73.3	76.5

(1) Pickup box. Also refer to Pickup Box Dimensions.
(2) The height data shown represents dimensions of a nominal vehicle with no options. Actual height may vary due to production tolerances.
(3) Add 3.4 inches for optional rear step bumper on Styleside models only.

FUEL TANK CAPACITY

Wheelbase	Availability	Location	Capacity (gallons)
F-150 119.9	Standard Tank	Midship	25.0
F-150 120.2	Standard Tank	Midship	24.5
F-150/F-250 138.5, 138.8	Standard Tank	Midship	30.0

CARGO VOLUME

Pickup Box (ft.)	Volume (cu. ft.)
F-150 6.5' Styleside	58.6
F-150/F-250 8.0' Styleside	72.6
F-150 6.5' Flareside	50.2

NOTE: Does not include allowances for wheelhouses.

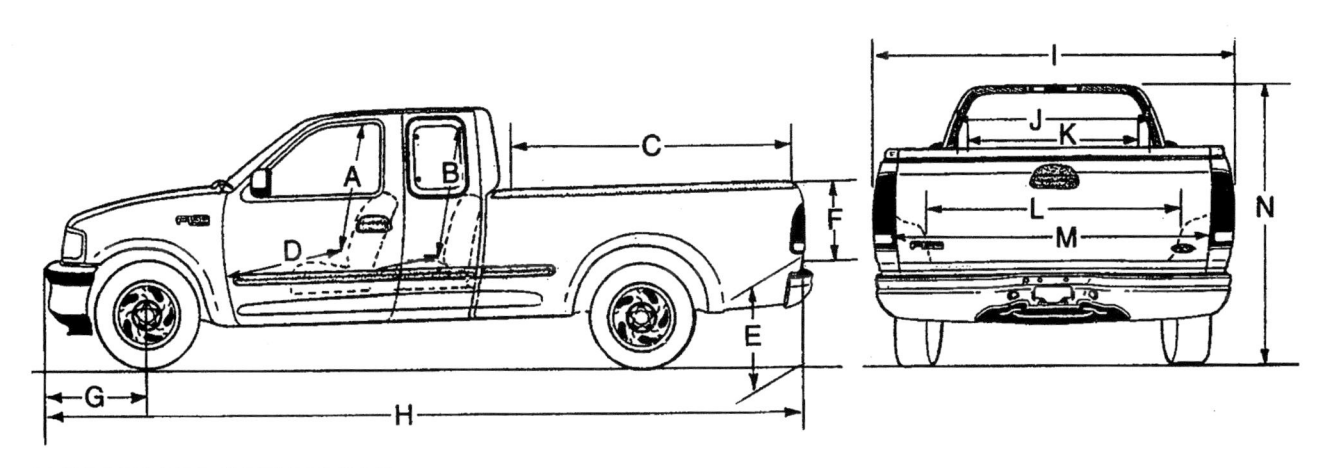

F-150/F-250 SUPERCAB

Code	Description	F-150 Styleside 4x2	4x4	4x2	4x4	F-150 Flareside 4x2	4x4	F-250 Styleside 4x2	4x4
	Model	F-150 Styleside				F-150 Flareside		F-250 Styleside	
	Drive	4x2		4x4		4x2	4x4	4x2	4x4
	Wheelbase (in.)	138.5	157.1	138.8	157.4	138.5	138.8	138.5	138.8
		Inches	Inches	Inches	Inches	Inches	Inches	Inches	Inches
A	Head Room (Front)	40.8	40.8	40.8	40.8	40.8	40.8	40.8	40.8
B	Head Room (Rear)	37.8	37.8	37.8	37.8	37.8	37.8	37.8	37.8
C	Inside Length[1]	78.8	97.0	78.8	97.0	78.8	78.8	78.8	78.8
D	Leg Room (Front)	40.9	40.9	40.9	40.9	40.9	40.9	40.9	40.9
	Leg Room (Rear)	32.2	32.2	32.2	32.2	32.2	32.2	32.2	32.2
E	Load Height (Empty)[2]	32.3	32.2	34.9	34.8	32.3	34.9	33.4	36.6
	Load Height (Loaded)[3]	26.4	26.5	29.7	29.8	26.4	29.7	27.1	30.7
F	Inside Height[2]	20.0	20.0	20.0	20.0	20.0	20.0	20.0	20.0
G	Front Overhang	37.2	37.2	38.7	38.7	37.2	38.7	37.2	38.7
H	Overall Length[3]	220.8	239.4	222.3	240.9	224.5	226.0	220.8	222.3
I	Width (Max.)	78.4	78.4	79.5	79.5	79.1	79.5	78.4	79.5
J	Shoulder Room (Front)	63.8	63.8	63.8	63.8	63.8	63.8	63.8	63.8
	Shoulder Room (Rear)	64.7	64.7	64.7	64.7	64.7	64.7	64.7	64.7
K	Hip Room (Front)	61.3	61.3	61.3	61.3	61.3	61.3	61.3	61.3
	Hip Room (Rear)	64.9	64.9	64.9	64.9	64.9	64.9	64.9	64.9
L	Width Between Wheelhouses[2]	50.0	50.0	50.0	50.0	50.0	50.0	50.0	50.0
M	Max. Load Width[2]	65.2	65.2	65.2	65.2	59.7	59.7	65.2	65.2
N	Cab Height (Empty)[3]	72.8	72.5	75.5	75.1	72.8	75.5	73.8	76.7

(1) Pickup box. Also refer to Pickup Box Dimensions.
(2) The height data shown represents dimensions of a nominal vehicle with no options. Actual height may vary due to production tolerances.
(3) Add 3.4" for optional rear step bumper on Styleside models only.

FUEL TANK CAPACITY

Wheelbase (in.)	Availability	Location	Capacity (gallons)
F-150/F-250 138.5, 138.8	Standard Tank	Midship	25.0
F-150 157.1/157.4	Standard Tank	Midship	30.0

CARGO VOLUME

Pickup Box (ft.)	Volume (cu. ft.)
F-150/F-250 6.5 Styleside	58.6
F-150 8.0 Styleside	72.6
F-150 6.5 Flareside	50.2

NOTE: Does not include allowances for wheelhouses.

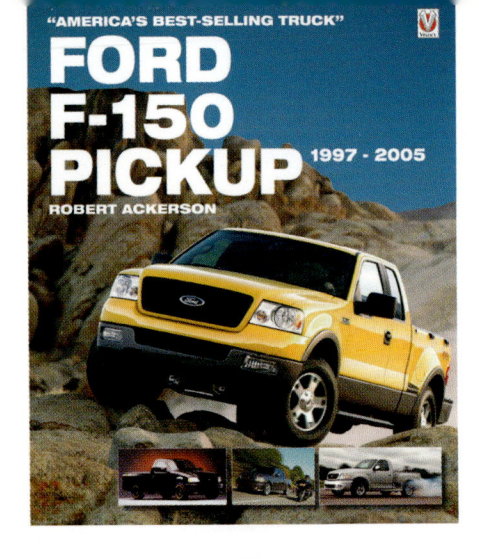

2
1998-2000

The 50th anniversary of Ford's F-series occurred on January 16, 1998. When the F-series was introduced in 1948, the F-150's direct ancestor, the F-1, was the smallest and lightest model offered.

The ½ ton (4700lb gross vehicle weight) F-1 was built on a 114in wheelbase and, with a standard 95hp, 6-cylinder 'Rouge 226' engine, listed for $1144. A 3-speed manual transmission with a floor shift was standard. A 4-speed gearbox was optional. With a 6.5ft bed, having a 454 sq-ft foot area, the F-1 pickup was depicted as the "Master of 1001 light delivery jobs". The F-1 was also offered in panel and flatbed styles. Shortly after the F-1 debuted, a 'Deluxe delivery' version, priced at $1367, and featuring "extra trim and styling", was offered. As an alternative to the standard 6-cylinder engine, which had been introduced in Ford's 1947 passenger cars, Ford's 100hp, 239 cubic inch flathead V-8, the 'Rouge 239', was available.

Integral to Ford's post-war recovery plan was the F-1's all-new styling which was deliberately intended to distinguish it from the previous model's prewar look. Instead of having fender-top-mounted headlights the F-1's were set flush into the fenders. The one-piece windshield improved visibility and gave the F-1 a streamlined look. Also contributing to the F-1's contemporary look were squared-off fenders, a larger rear window, and side-vent windows.

Ford spent one million dollars designing the cabs of its new trucks. No surprise then, that it was called the 'Million Dollar Cab'. The F-1 was first and foremost, still a truck, but its interior was no longer structured along strictly utilitarian lines. At 65in, it was 7in wider than its predecessors. A new ventilation system provided three-way fresh air control. The optional, dealer-installed, 'Magic-Air' fresh air heater and defroster used hot water from the engine to warm outside air as it was pulled into the cab. The coil spring bench seat could be inclined rearward, adjusted in height, and had a 3in fore-and-aft adjustment range. An optional single driver's seat, the "Spiralounge Seat", had a special hydraulic shock absorber and spring that could be

The famous photo of a pre-production 1948 F-1 model at Ford's Highland Park plant. (Courtesy of Ford Division Public Affairs)

A 1998 F-150 Lariat poses with a 1948 F-1 owned by David Marquart of Akron, NY. The Lariat is the 50th Anniversary Special Edition F-series, a limited edition Lariat SuperCab with a gold trim package. It went on sale in April 1998. In addition to the Vermilion finish of this F-1, the 1948 models were also available in Meadow Green, Black, Birch Gray, and Yellow. (Courtesy of Ford Division Public Affairs)

adjusted to the driver's weight. Along with wider doors, increased head and leg room, and easier to read instruments, the F-1 also favorably impressed customers with features such as a sun visor and ashtray.

Additional refinements making the F-1 more comfortable than past models included a new suspension system using rubber pads and rubber insulated bolts to reduce the impact of bumps, engine vibrations, and road noise upon the occupants.

A series of *Saturday Evening Post* advertisements maximized the F-1's exposure to a truck market characterized by pent-up demand and enthusiasm for something new to drive. One focus of these full-page advertisements was that buyers got more for their money since the new truck was "Bonus Built". Joining this value for money theme were assurances that the new trucks were tough and reliable. Statements such as "Built Stronger to Last Longer" were backed up with testimonials from insurance experts that the new Fords will "last up to 19.6% longer", and estimates that they would have a ten-year lifespan, which, in 1948, was considered long for work vehicles.

Helping potential customers connect with the new model were several full-page 'Smart Idea' advertisements featuring real-life stories about companies successfully using the new Ford trucks. One of the most widely circulated photos of the 1948 F-1 showed a pre-production model parked in front of Ford's Highland Park plant being loaded with heavy cargo.

F-series production began at Ford's assembly plants at Norfolk, Virginia and Atlanta, Georgia. It quickly expanded to fourteen other plants. The F-1's numerous features and what proved to be classic styling made it a favorite of farmers, small-business owners, tradesmen, commercial fleet operators, and many government agencies.

Total production for 1948

The 1998 F-150 XLT Regular Cab in Light Prairie Tan Clearcoat Metallic. (Author's collection)

Below: A 1998 F-150 SuperCab XLT Flareside 4x4. (Courtesy of Ford Division Public Affairs)

was 290,000; Ford's highest truck production level since 1929. Half a century later, Ford reported domestic sales of 836,629 F-series pickups, making them the best selling trucks for the 20th straight year. Moreover, by 1998, the F-series was the bestselling vehicle in the US - car or truck - for the 17th consecutive year. Three years earlier, in 1995, the F-series had surpassed the Volkswagen Beetle as the bestselling nameplate of all-time. Perhaps the most incredible tribute to the F-1's place in Ford history was the fact that one of every ten vehicles sold since Ford was founded in 1903 had been an F-series Truck. When Ford celebrated its 100th anniversary in 2003, the F-series trucks were voted by the global automotive media as one of Ford's twenty-five most significant products.

As in 1997, the F-150 for 1998 was offered in both regular cab and extended cab bodies with either a Styleside or Flareside box. The F-150's four trim levels (Standard, XL, XLT, and Lariat) were retained, but many changes in options, features, and package content were made. Two new exterior Clearcoat Metallic colors, Silver and Light Denim Blue, replaced Silver Frost and Portofino Blue. Clearcoat Metallic Colors carried over from 1997 were Light Prairie Tan, Dark Toreador Red, Moonlight Blue, Pacific Green, and Teal. Clearcoat colors continued from 1997 were Bright Red, Black, and Oxford White. As in 1997, four interior trim colors were available: Cordovan, Willow Green, Medium Graphite, and Medium Prairie Tan.

All 1998 F-series models had a 50th anniversary logo depicting a 1948 pickup along side a 1998 truck. The logo appeared on the rear window of the driver's side.

Triton V-8 badging was added to the front quarter panels on all F-150s with V-8 engines. Added to the content of Lariat models were outside power signal mirrors and a color-keyed (Medium Graphite or Medium Prairie Tan) leather wrapped steering wheel.

Offered as a 'Limited Availability' XL option was a 40/60 split bench with driver's lumbar. The passenger manual lumbar support previously installed on Captain's Chairs was deleted. Lumbar support for the driver's seat was continued.

The color-keyed floor mats used on the 1997 XL were replaced by black vinyl units. Several features included in the content of the 1997 Standard and XL models were now optional. These consisted of the cargo box light, tailgate key lock, and tow hooks. Flip-out quarter glass windows previously included on Standard/XL SuperCabs became an option. The door activated illuminated entry system formerly standard on the XLT and Lariats models became part of the remote keyless entry option. Also moved into the option category was the two-tone paint that had been standard on the Lariat.

18

This 1998 F-150 Lariat SuperCab has a Pacific Green Clearcoat Metallic/Light Prairie Tan color combination. (Author's collection)

All models had second generation (depowered) air bags, improved door hatches for easier egress, and door trim panels with improved soil resistance. A redesign of the exterior door latch improved its accessibility. More obvious was the F-150's relocated exhaust pipe which was moved from the front to the rear of the back wheel. This was not a cosmetic change since Ford reported that it resulted in improved cold-weather performance.

A new STX package was offered for 4x2 XLT Regular Cab pickups powered by the 4.2L V-6 or 4.6L V-8 engine. Content consisted of an 'STX' decal, 4x4 grille insert with color-keyed grille surround, color-keyed 4x2 front and rear bumpers, color-keyed power mirrors, cast aluminum wheels, P275/60R17 All-Season BSW tires, and a 3.55:1 rear axle ratio. Three Clearcoat Metallic colors were offered: Bright Red, Black, and Oxford White. This option could be installed on both Styleside and Flareside models.

All F-150 models were available with LT 245/74Rx16D tires if severe use was anticipated. During the model year, fog lamps, earlier standard for 4x4 Lariats, became optional for all 4x4 models. Similarly, a heavy-duty electrical/cooling package joined the 'delayed availability' option list for all models. It contained 72 Amp-hr battery, heavy-duty 130 Amp alternator (4.2 liter engine only, already standard on V-8), super engine cooling, auxiliary transmission oil cooler (with automatic transmission only), and engine oil cooler with 5.4 liter V-8. Phased in during the model year was a carpet delete option for the XLT and Lariat, and a rear storage bin for Standard and XL F-150s.

Appealing to customers interested in using alternative fuels was a bi-fuel engine prep package for use with natural gas or propane and regular gas. A dual in-bed natural gas/propane fuel tank was also optional. Both the Standard and XL models could now be ordered with a Pickup Box Security Group consisting of a tailgate lock and integral cargo/box light. Tow hooks became optional for Standard and XL 4x4 models. Chrome styled steel wheels were available for XL Flaresides. Standard and XL SuperCabs could be ordered with the flip-out rear windows. All-terrain P235/70Rx16SL (BSW or OWL) tires were no longer available.

The Heavy-Duty Service package was replaced by two new option packages; the previously noted Heavy-Duty Electrical/Cooling package and a Snow Plow Prep package. Content of the latter included the Heavy-Duty Electrical/Cooling package, P255/70Rx16SL OWL, all-terrain tires (including spare tire), 3.55:1 rear axle, styled steel wheels (Standard and XL), chrome styled wheels (XLT), heavy-duty shock absorbers, and front GAWR upgrade to 3900lb. Ford recommended the Regular Cab 4x4 Styleside long wheelbase F-150 model with the 5.4 liter engine and automatic transmission for installation of the Snow Plow Prep package.

Ford and NASCAR marked the 50th anniversary of the F-series truck and NASCAR's creation by agreeing to a five year contract designating Ford as the official truck of NASCAR. Ford trucks were highly visible both as the official truck for NASCAR's racing divisions and as its inspection and support vehicles, but the real attention-grabber was the limited production NASCAR Edition F-150. After debuting at the Chicago Auto Show in February 1998, NASCAR Edition production began in mid-May 1998 and was reported by Ford as limited to 3000 units. All were manufactured at Ford's Norfolk, Virginia truck assembly plant. Order code 94N was assigned to the NASCAR Special Edition F-150.

The NASCAR Edition was promoted regionally, as a package, primarily for Ford's dealers in the southeast where NASCAR was extremely popular. "This Limited-Edition Vehicle", said Ford, "is offered to select regions to be the centerpiece for FAAF and dealership promotions in the July through September time frame."

Not surprisingly, the first official order was placed by Jim France, NASCAR's executive vice president. The transaction took place in Daytona Beach at Gary Yoemans Ford, located near Daytona International Speedway.

In announcing the NASCAR Edition, Ford explained, "NASCAR racing is hot! It continues to grow with ever-increasing attendance and TV audiences. And 1998 is a huge year for NASCAR-and F-series. It marks the 50th anniversary of both.

"To celebrate this relationship, we are proud to introduce an exciting new limited edition F-series Pickup - the 1998 NASCAR Special Edition F-150. Its unique, lowered, racy look, plus official NASCAR identification creates a bold, distinctive image that will have

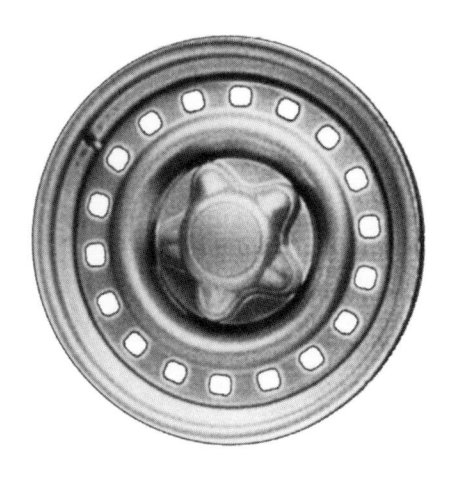

The base wheel for the 1998 Standard and XL F-150 was this 16 x 7in Argent painted steel wheel with an Argent hub. (Author's collection)

Offered only as an option for the 1998 XLT F-150 was this polished aluminum 16 x7in wheel with a chrome hub. (Author's collection)

The 1998 Lariat F-150's standard 16 x 7in cast aluminum wheel with a chrome hub. It was also optional for the XLT. (Author's collection)

The 16x 7in chrome styled steel wheel that was optional for XL Flareside models, and included with Payload Package #3, LT245/75R 16D BSW All-Season tires and the Snow Plow Prep Package. (Author's collection)

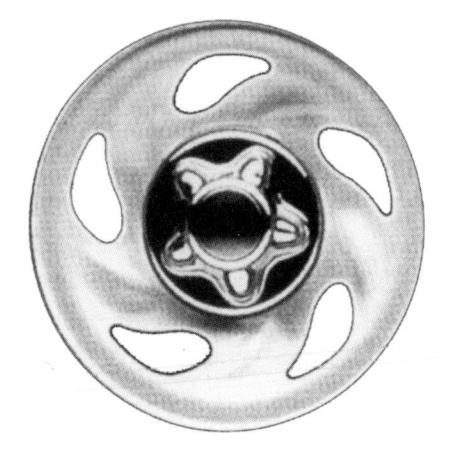

Standard for the 1998 XLT and optional for the XL was this 16 x 7in Argent styled steel wheel with a chrome hub. Also, it was optional for the XL and included and available only for the Standard models as part of the optional for 4x2 139in wheelbase Regular Cabs. It was both a separate option for the XL and part of the XL's Payload Package #3. (Author's collection)

The cast aluminum 17 x 7.5in wheel with a chrome center that was included in the 4x4 Off-Road Equipment Group for 1998. This option was available for the XL, XLT, and Lariat F-150s. (Author's collection)

The 1998 NASCAR Edition F-150 had yellow-lettered Goodyear tires, a Roush front air dam, and 10-spoke black aluminum wheels. (Courtesy of Ford Media Services)

Unlike this prototype, the production model NASCAR Edition F-150 had its exhausts exiting behind the right rear wheel. (Courtesy of Ford Media Services)

21

strong appeal for NASCAR fans."

The NASCAR Edition was based on the 120in wheelbase, 2WD regular cab, F-150 with a short box. Only one engine was offered; the 220 horsepower, 4.6 liter Triton V-8 engine. A unique 3.73:1 axle ratio was used and towing capacity was rated at 2000 pounds. Either a 5-speed manual or 4-speed automatic overdrive transmission could be selected.

The distinctive appearance of the NASCAR Edition combined a jet black exterior with special box sides and tailgate NASCAR graphics. Except for an XLT grille insert, the NASCAR Edition used XL trim appointments. Yellow lettered Goodyear Wrangler P255/70R16 AP tires were mounted on 16x7in ten-spoke black aluminum wheels. Overall height was reduced by one inch. Parts supplier Roush provided a front air dam, exhaust system and dual stainless steel exhaust tips. The use of the dual outlets, with their reduced back pressure necessitated the use of a new FOU1 computer code for the engine. When the NASCAR Edition prototype was displayed at the Chicago Show in 1998, its dual exhaust tips exited just ahead of the right side rear wheel. They were moved behind the wheel on production models.

A gray cloth 60/40 bench seat with a center arm rest was specified. Both the headrests and floor mats carried the NASCAR logo. The dash contained the gauge package with a tachometer. Aside from an automatic transmission, four other options were offered including a tonneau cover originally planned as a 1999 model year option. Supply of the tonneau was limited as Ford reported it was available only for 600 of the trucks produced.

The F-150's exterior changes for 1999, if not extensive, were readily

F-150 model and option prices (1998)

Model	MSRP*
Styleside 4x2 Regular Cab	
120in wb, Standard	$14,835
120in wb, XL	$15,865
120in wb, XLT	$18,465
120in wb, Lariat	$20.900
139in wb, Standard	$15,125
139in wb, XL	$16,165
139in wb, XLT	$18,765
139in wb, Lariat	$21,200
Flareside 4x2 Regular Cab	
120in wb, XL	$16,875
120in wb, XLT	$19,475
120in wb, Lariat	$21,200
Styleside 4x4 Regular Cab	
120in wb, Standard	$18,055
120in wb, XL	$19,205
120in wb, XLT	$21.640
120in wb, Lariat	$24,075
139in wb, Standard	$18,345
139in wb, XL	$19,505
139in wb, XLT	$21,940
139in wb, Lariat	$24,375
Flareside 4x4 Regular Cab	
120in wb, XL	$19,970
120in wb, XLT	$22,405
120in wb, Lariat	$24,840
Styleside 4x2 SuperCab	
139in wb, Standard	$17,140
139in wb, XL	$18,380
139in wb, XLT	$21,200
139in wb, Lariat	$23,655
157in wb, Standard	$17,430
157in wb, XL	$18,680
157in wb, XLT	$21,520
157in wb, Lariat	$23,955

continued next page

22

Model	MSRP*
Flareside 4x2 SuperCab	
139in wb, XL	$19,140
139in wb, XLT	$21,980
139in wb, Lariat	$24,415
Styleside 4x4 SuperCab	
139in wb, Standard	$20,760
139in wb, XL	$22,130
139in wb, XLT	$24,930
139in wb, Lariat	$26,730
157in wb, Standard	$21,050
157in wb, XL	$22,430
157in wb, XLT	$25,230
157in wb, Lariat	$27,030
Flareside 4x4 SuperCab	
139in wb, XL	$22,770
139in wb, XLT	$25,615
139in wb, Lariat	$27,415

*Destination and Delivery charge was an additional $640.

Options	Price
Engine	
4.6 liter V-8	$635
5.4 liter V-8 Lariat and SuperCab	$665
All others	$1300
5.4 liter Bi-Fuel Prep. System Lariat (Reg. Cab only)	$815
All others (Reg. Cab only)	$1450
Electronic Automatic Overdrive Trans.	$995
Limited slip rear axle	$260
Optional axle ratio Upgrade	$50
Limited slip with Optional axle ratio Upgrade	$310
Payload Packages	
Payload Package #2	$50
Payload Package #3 Standard trim	$470
XL & XLT trim	$270
California Emissions System	$170
Tires (depending on size and model)	$125-$715
Seats	
Standard	
Poly-Knit Bench	$100
SuperCab rear seat	$415
XL	
Vinyl Bench	(-$100)
40/60 Split Bench	$150
XLT	
Captain's Chairs with console	$490
Lariat	
Leather Captain's Chairs with console	$490
Four-wheel ABS	$500
4x4 Off-Road Equipment Group	
Lariat	$745
XLT	$1145
Air Conditioning	$805
Painted rear step bumper (Standard trim)	$100
Chrome rear step bumper (XL trim)	$150
Cab steps, Regular Cab	$320
Cab steps, SuperCab	$370
Carpet Delete	
Lariat trim (includes floor mats delete)	(-$100) continued over

Options	Price
XLT trim	(-$50)
Floor carpeting with XLT trim	$100
Electric shift-on-the-fly 4x4 (XL & Lariat only)	$150
Heavy-Duty Electrical/Cooling Package	$210
Reg. Cab carpeted floor mats (color-keyed on XLT)	$30
SuperCab front and rear carpeted floor mats (color-keyed on XLT)	$50
Fog Lamps (4x4 only)	$140
Fuel System Natural Gas (Bi-Fuel)	$5810
Fuel System Propane (Bi-Fuel)	$4950
Fuel System In-Bed Dual w/66N (Bi-Fuel)	$1280
Fuel System In-Bed Dual w/66P (Bi-Fuel)	$135
Privacy Glass (SuperCab XL only)	$100
Engine Black Heater	$90
Lower two-tone paint (XLT/Lariat only)	$190
Pickup Box Security Group	$45
Power Driver's Seat/Autolamp (XLT/Lariat only)	$360
Remote Keyless Entry/Anti-Theft (XLT/Lariat only)	$265
Skid Plates (Reg. Cab SWB 4x4)	$80
Skid Plates (all other 4x4 models)	$160
Snow Plow Prep Package (Std/XL/XLT, LWB Reg. Cab 4x4 only)	$505
Speed Control/Tilt Steering Wheel	$385
Rear Storage Bin (Reg. cab only)	$90

apparent. Both the front bumper system and bodyside molding were restyled as were the optional 16in cast aluminum wheels.

All SuperCab models had a standard fourth door for increased ease of rear seat entry and exit as well as easier access to the rear cargo area. On both sides of the truck, the front door had to be opened before the rear door could be opened. An interior latch handle was mounted on the door trim panel. The door was hinged at the back, adding to the accessibility of the rear area.

XLT series trucks were available with a new optional single CD stereo radio with speed compensated volume control. Also new was a premium stereo radio with speed compensated volume control offered with either the single CD or 6-disc changer option. The XLT's stereo radio option was deleted. P235/70R16 A/S OWL tires were added to the XL series option list. Privacy glass with flip-open rear quarter windows were now grouped together as an option for SuperCab, XLT, and Lariat models.

A new Convenience Group was standard for the XLT and optional for the XL. Major elements included speed control with tap up/down feature, five-position tilt steering wheel, lockable tailgate, and cargo light.

Additional new standard features of the XLT series consisted of polished aluminum wheels, AM/FM stereo cassette radio, covered rear storage bin (delete option available), power exterior rear view mirrors, air conditioning, and for 4x4 models, fog lamps. Two new items; styled steel wheels and a SuperCab rear seat (delete option available) were added to the standard equipment of the XL.

Numerous options previously offered for the XL were deleted for the 1999 models, including the vinyl bench seat, chromed styled steel wheels, cab steps, rear storage bin for the Regular Cab, flip-open rear quarter vent windows, and privacy glass.

Replacing the Standard Series in the 1999 F-150 lineup was a new Work Series. Standard Series options that weren't carried over for the Work trucks included cloth full bench seat, stereo cassette radio, fog lamps, Pickup Box Security Group, flip-open rear quarter vent window (SuperCab),

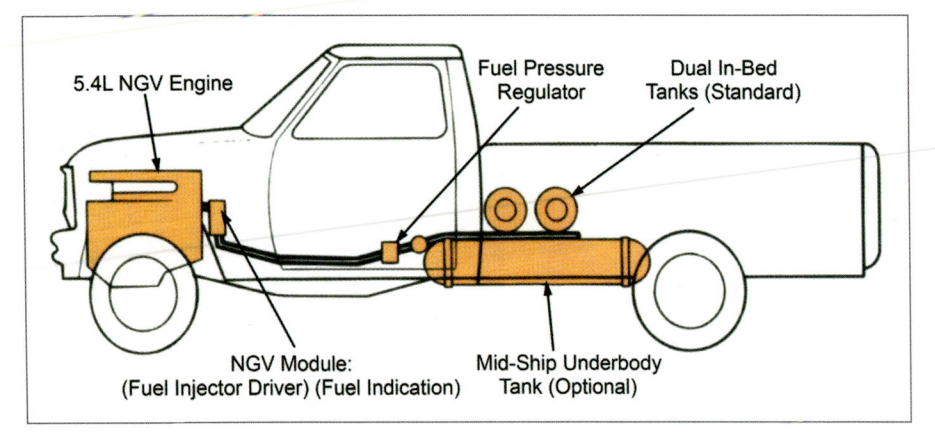

The dedicated natural gas 1998 F-150 was based on the Regular Cab 4x2 model. It was fitted with a 5.4 liter Triton V-8 developing 195 horsepower, an electronic 4-speed automatic overdrive transmission, and rear wheel anti-lock brakes. Ford reported it was capable of meeting California's Super Ultra Low Emission Vehicle standards. Since the 1990 Clear Air Act, Ford had sold more alternative fuel vehicles in the US than all other automakers combined. (Author's collection)

The Standard F-150's vinyl bench seat for 1998. A poly-knit version was standard for the XL and optional for the Standard F-150. The XL could also be ordered with the vinyl upholstery. Available colors were Medium Graphite and Medium Prairie Tan. (Author's collection)

P255/70R16 A/T OWl tires, front tow hooks (4x4), rear storage bin (Regular Cab), and cab steps. A painted rear step bumper was standard for the Work Series.

The 4x4 Off-Road Package now included new 17in chromed steel wheels with new 17in light truck tires suitable for severe usage conditions. A 3.73:1 axle ratio was used with the 5.4 liter engine.

Debuting in 1999 was a new 4x4 Package with P265/70R17 A/T OWL tires, 17in sport aluminum wheels and a '4x4' decal. A 3.55:1 axle ratio was specified for models with the 4.2 and 4.6 liter engines. A 3.54:1 ratio was used with the 5.4 liter engine.

Lariat series revisions began with restyled Lariat lettering and tape stripes. Added to its standard equipment was a six-way power 40/60 leather split bench seat, remote keyless entry, a single CD stereo radio with speed compensated volume control, and, for Regular Cabs, a rear storage bin. OWL all-terrain tires were standard for 4x4 Lariats. Only an automatic transmission was available for the Lariat.

The Snow Plow Prep Group's front gross axle weight rating was increased from 3700lb to 3900lb. By increasing the 4.6 liter V-8's Gross Vehicle Weight to over 6000lb which represented an additional 100lb-300lb payload capacity, it became possible for that engine to be ordered with the Snow Plow Prep Group. Aluminum wheels with increased weight ratings were available with the V8 Payload Package #3. The perimeter anti-theft used in 1998 was replaced by a SecuriLock anti-theft system with improved vehicle theft protection.

The standard 40/60 split bench seat with manual driver's side lumbar support for the 1998 XLT F-150. It was also optional for the XL; the center storage was a separate option for the XL. Color selection consisted of Cordovan, Willow Green, Medium Graphite, and Medium Prairie Tan. (Author's collection)

The 1998 Lariat F-150 had this standard 40/60 split bench seat with manual driver's side lumbar support and leather surfaces. Two colors, Medium Graphite and Medium Prairie Tan, were available. (Author's collection)

These Captain's Chairs with console and manual driver's side lumbar support were optional for both the 1998 XLT and Lariat F-150. The XLT version had cloth trim, the Lariat's had leather seating surfaces. The color selection was limited to Medium Graphite and Medium Prairie Tan. (Author's collection)

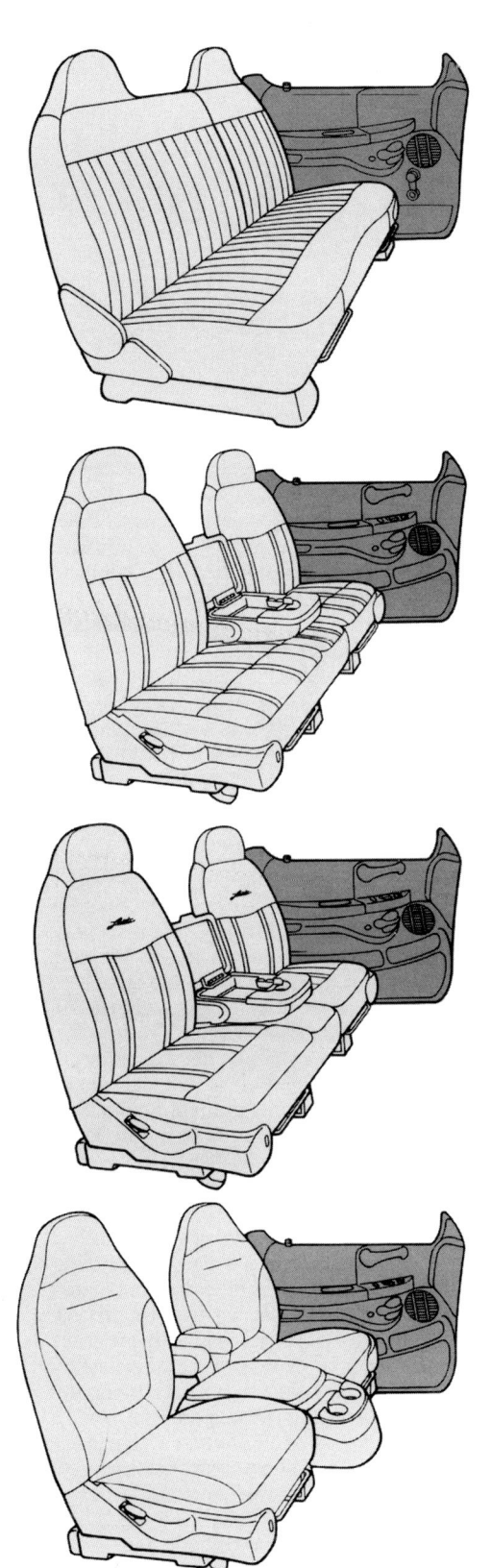

25

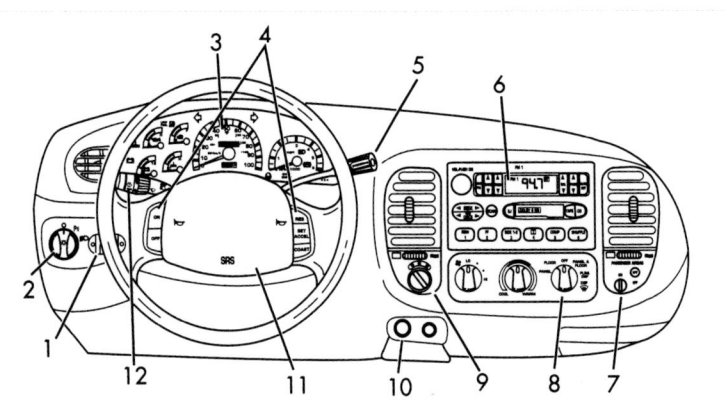

1. Instrument panel dimmer switch
2. Headlamp control
3. Speedometer
4. Speed control[1]
5. Automatic transmission gearshift lever with overdrive lockout switch[1]
6. Audio system controls
7. Passenger airbag deactivation switch
8. Climate controls
9. 4WD control[1]
10. Auxiliary power point
11. Driver airbag
12. Turn signal, washer control and high-beam switch

(1) If equipped.

The arrangement of the 1999 F-150 instrument panel. (Author's collection)

Major changes took place in the F-150's exterior color selection. No longer offered were four Clearcoat Metallic colors: Pacific Green, Moonlight Blue, Light Denim Blue, and Light Prairie Tan. Four new Clearcoat Metallic colors were added: Amazon Green, Deep Wedgewood Blue, Harvest Gold, and Toreador Red.

Carried over from 1998 were Bright Red Clearcoat, Dark Toreador Red Clearcoat Metallic, Teal Clearcoat Metallic, Black Clearcoat and Silver Clearcoat Metallic. Eliminated from the F-150's interior color choices were Cordovan and Willow Green. They were replaced by Dark Graphite and Denim Blue. Medium Graphite, and Medium Prairie Tan remained available.

New door trim panels added to the interior's usable space and improved the ergonomics of the functional controls. The front seats were restyled for improved comfort and appearance. A more durable and longer lasting carpet was installed, providing what Ford depicted as "improved visual appearance". All headliners were now color-coordinated. A new green interior lighting color was also introduced.

The factory installed tonneau cover that was part of the 1998 NASCAR Edition F-150 package was offered for all 1999 models. Aside from such aspects as visual appeal, cargo protection, and security this option also improved fuel economy. Another all-new option for 1999 was tubular running boards. Installation was limited to 4x4 Stylesides and 4x2/4x4 Flaresides.

Ford linked axle ratio usage in 1999 with tire selections to address what was depicted as "performance feel issues". A new 3.73:1 axle ratio was offered for trucks with the 5.4 liter V-8 and 17in tires. The horsepower rating of the 5.4 liter V-8 for 1999 to 260@4500rpm, which represented an increase of 25 horsepower over the previous rating. Its maximum torque was now 345lb/ft@2300rpm or 15lb/ft more than in 1998.

Having offered Lightning models in the 1993-1995 model years, Ford's introduction of a new version, officially designated the 1999 Ford SVT F-150 Lightning, was welcomed by performance truck enthusiasts. John Coletti, special vehicle engineering manager, gave potential owners ample grounds for high expectations. "Our customers will enjoy the highest performance pickup truck ever built. The 1999 SVT F-150 Lightning will not only accelerate like a bolt from the blue, it will stop in a flash, and ride and handle like no other pickup before it."

The latest Lightning, which was displayed at the March, 1998 Chicago auto show, was based on the F-150 Regular Cab XLT Flareside 2x4 model. Cobra-style driving lights were used along with special rocker and rear panels. The front fascia was modified to improve engine cooling. As were the rocker panel moldings, both the front and rear fascias were body-colored. The dual exhausts exited just ahead of the right side rear wheels.

Compared to a stock F-150's, the Lightning suspension was ½in lower in the front and 2in lower in the rear. A rear anti-roll bar was used along with uniquely tuned springs and gas charged shock absorbers. Five-leaf, 200lb/in rear springs replaced the standard three leaf setup. SVT coil springs rated at 650lb/in were used at the front. Disc brakes from the larger and heavier F-250 were used as the starting point for the Lightning's four-wheel disc brake system. Vented discs with a 12.1in diameter and twin-piston calipers were used at the front. The rear solid rotors measured 13.1in in diameter and had single-piston calipers. Both sets had rotors

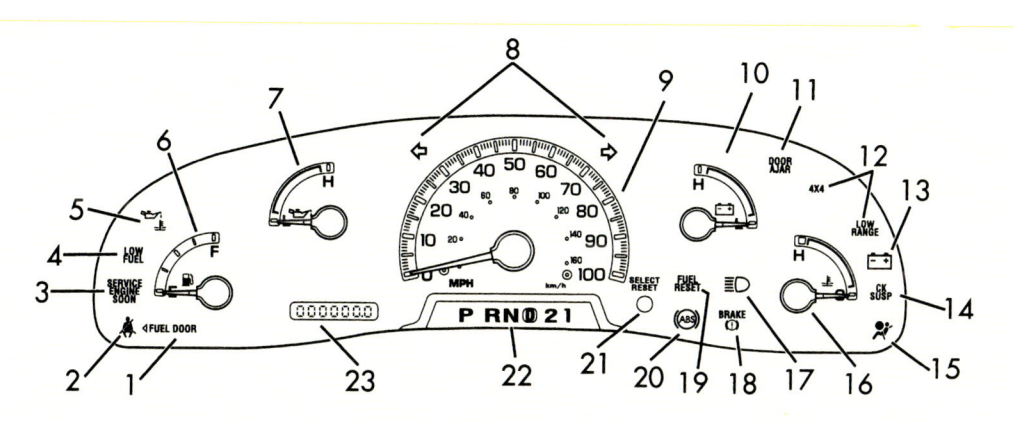

1. Fuel door location reminder
2. Fasten safety belt warning light
3. Service engine soon light
4. Low fuel warning light
5. Oil pressure warning light
6. Fuel gauge
7. Engine oil pressure gauge
8. Turn signal indicators
9. Speedometer
10. Voltmeter
11. Door ajar warning light
12. 4x4 indicator lights[1]
13. Charging system warning light
14. Check air suspension light[1]
15. Airbag readiness indicator/ warning light
16. Engine coolant temperature gauge
17. High-beam indicator
18. Brake system warning light/ parking brake
19. Fuel pump inertia shutoff switch indicator
20. Anti-lock Braking System warning light
21. Trip odometer select/reset button
22. Automatic transmission gearshift indicator[1]
23. Trip odometer

(1) If equipped.

Identification of the 1999 F-150 instrumentation cluster. (Author's collection)

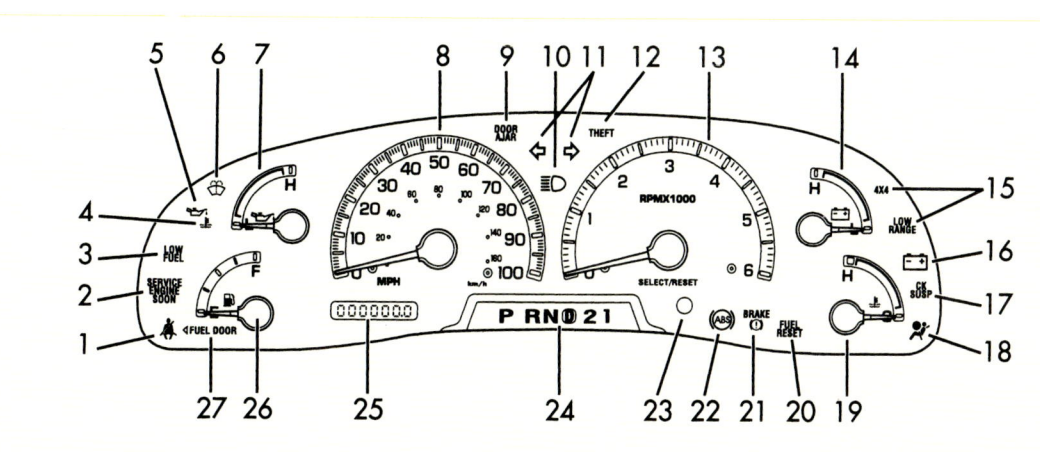

1. Fasten safety belt warning light
2. Service engine soon warning light
3. Low fuel light
4. Engine coolant temperature warning light
5. Oil pressure warning light
6. Low windshield washer fluid light
7. Engine oil pressure gauge
8. Speedometer
9. Door ajar light
10. High beam indicator light
11. Turn signal indicators
12. Anti-theft security system warning light
13. Tachometer
14. Battery voltage gauge
15. 4x4 system indicators[1]
16. Electrical service warning light
17. Check air suspension light[1]
18. Airbag service light
19. Engine coolant temperature gauge
20. Fuel pump inertia shutoff switch reset light
21. Low brake fluid/parking brake light
22. Anti-lock Braking System warning light
23. Trip odometer/odometer select/ reset button
24. Automatic transmission gear selection display
25. Trip odometer/odometer display
26. Fuel gauge
27. Fuel door location reminder

(1) If equipped.

Details of the tachometer cluster option available for the 1999 F-150. (Author's collection)

27

4mm thicker than the stock F-150 units. A 4-wheel, three-channel ABS system was standard. five-spoke cast alloy wheels measuring 18x9.5in were fitted with P295/45ZR-18 Goodyear Eagle F1GS tires. Ford claimed that the Lightning stopped in 137 feet from 60mph. Only one power train was offered, a supercharged and intercooled 5.4 liter Triton V-8 (the first supercharged V-8 ever offered for a pickup), rated at 360hp@4750rpm and 440lb/ft of torque@3000rpm, and a 4-speed automatic, essentially a Ford 4R100 diesel transmission used for Ford's turbocharged diesel pickups, strengthened by a heavy-duty torque converter. A 9.75in limited slip rear axle with a 3.551 ratio was specified as was an engine oil cooler and super engine cooling and auxiliary transmission cooler packages.

Lightning engine assembly began on January 14, 1999 on the low volume line (LVL) at Ford's Windsor, Ontario Engine Plant Annex. Officials of Ford's Special Vehicle Team and Roush Engineering, which designed the engine, watched as the assembly of the first two dozen of an expected six-year total of 24,000 Lightning engines was completed.

Lightning production began at Ford's Oakville, Ontario Truck Plant (OPT) in early March, 1999. The plant manager, Charles Shortridge, was obviously pleased: "The selection of OPT as the sole manufacturing plant for the Lightning is a fitting tribute to the highly skilled, talented, and dedicated work force at this plant. It is also a confirmation of the over one billion dollar investment in OPT made by Ford Motor Company to expand the plant for the introduction of the 1997 F-series pickup truck".

Lightning specifications

Engine	
Type	90-degree Triton V-8
Construction	Cast iron block, aluminum-alloy cylinder heads
Borexstroke	3.55in (90mm) x 4.16in (105.6mm)
Displacement	330cu in (5386cc)
Compression ratio	8.4:1
Valve train	Single overhead cam, chain drive, roller finger followers with hydraulic lash adjustment, beehive valve springs
Intake valve	44.5mm head diameter
Exhaust valve	36mm head diameter
Fuel system	Sequential electronic fuel injection
Induction system	Pressure-charged with Eaton Gen.IV Roots-type supercharger, water-to-air intercooler
Max. boost pressure	8.0psi
Throttle body	Dual-bore 57mm
Mass-air sensor	90mm dia
Exhaust system	Cast iron headers, tuned dual exhaust (dual catalytic converters and Walker mufflers) with ceramic-coated dual exhaust tips
Horsepower	360@4750rpm
Torque	440lb/ft@3000rpm
Redline	5250rpm (fuel shut-off at 5400rpm)
Transmission	4R100, 4-speed automatic with lockup torque converter
Ratios	
First	2.71
Second	1.53
Third	1.00
Fourth	0.71
Reverse	2.176
Axle Ratio	3.55:1, limited slip differential
Suspension	
Front	Independent, unequal length control arms, coil springs, tubular gas-charged shock absorbers, 31mm solid anti-roll bar.
Rear	Solid axle, five leaf semi-elliptical springs, staggered gas-charged shock absorbers, 23mm solid anti-roll bar
Steering	Recirculating ball, power assisted
Ratio	14.0:1
Turns lock-to-lock	3.3
Turning circle	44.3ft (curb-to-curb)
Brakes	Power assist vacuum with 4-wheel ABS, three-sensor system
Front	12.1inx ½in Vented disc, twin piston caliper
Rear	13.1inx0.6in vented disc, single piston caliper
Wheels	9.5inx18in cast aluminum
Tires	Goodyear Eagle F1-GSTM, P295/45ZR-18, 235/70R-16 spare tire

Lightnings were available only through the approximately 620 SVT-certified Ford dealers. But before appearing in these showrooms, the Lightning became familiar to millions of NASCAR fans as the official pace vehicle of the Winston Cup Cracker Barrel 500 race at Atlanta Motor Speedway.

"We're pleased that Ford Division chose the SVT F-150 Lightning as the

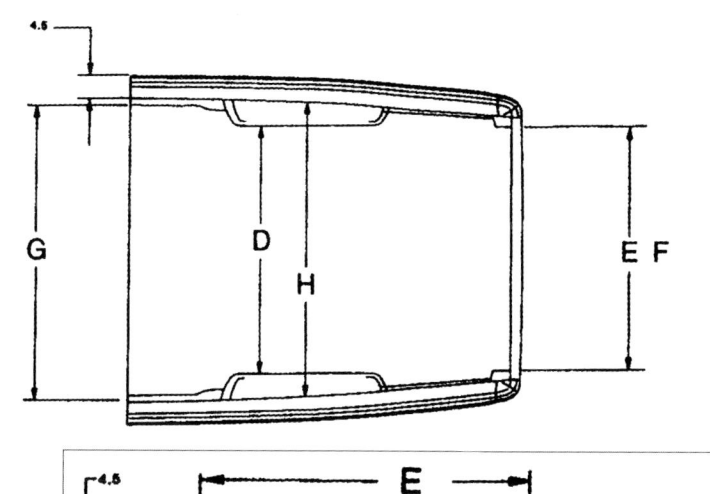

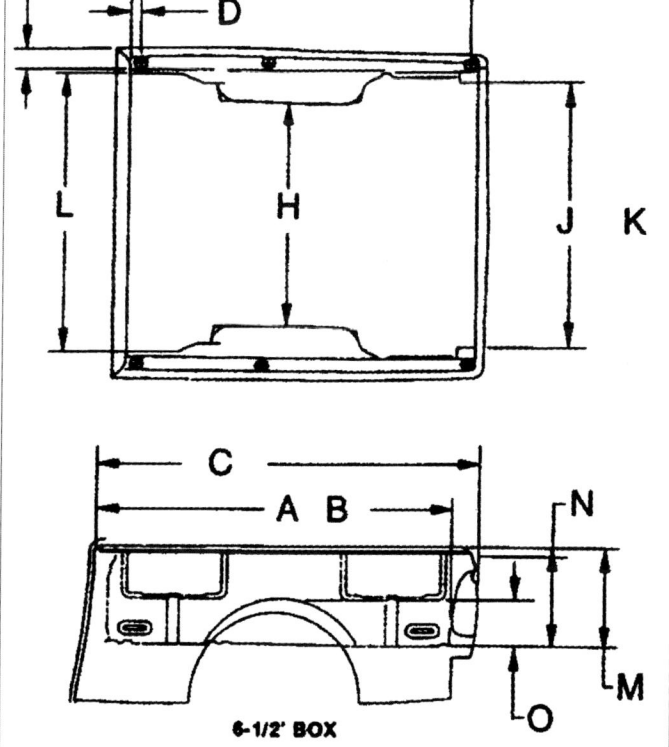

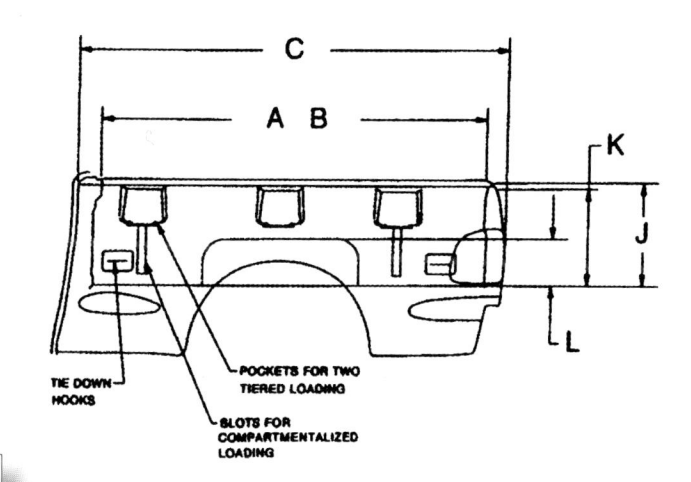

The dimensions of the three pickup boxes offered for the 1999 F-150 varied from model to model. (Author's collection)

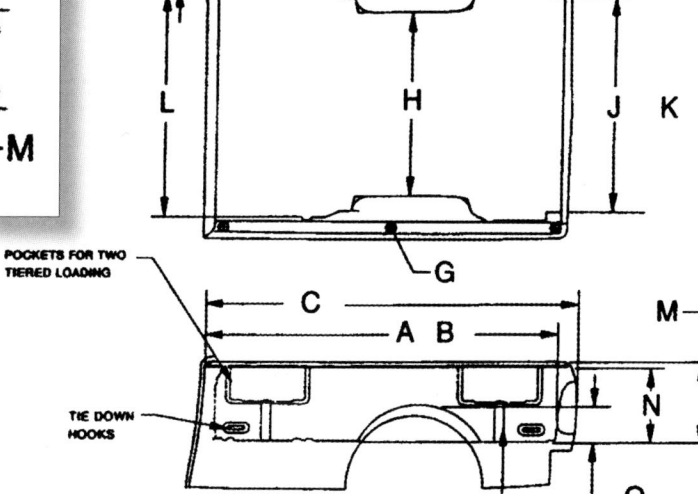

pace vehicle for the Cracker Barrel 500", said Tom Scarpello, specialty vehicle marketing manager. "We think it shows that the Lightning is just as much at home on the track as on the street. The Lightning outperforms many sports cars on the road today, and of course, it packs all the toughness you expect in a Ford truck."

Three exterior Clearcoat colors were available: Bright Red, Black, and

29

Oxford White. Only a single interior, Medium Graphite Harris suede cloth with textured Ebony accents and leather door trim was offered. The Lightning's seats were based on the F-150 40/60 split bench seat, to which were added side and seat back bolsters, and a six-way power driver's seat. A large fold down armrest contained a storage area and two large cup holders.

The Lightning's four-spoke tilt steering wheel was leather wrapped and had a thicker section-width rim. The SVT 'sport instrument panel' consisted of electroluminescent white-faced gauges with orange needles for fuel, oil temperature, 140mph speedometer, 6000rpm tachometer, with 5250rpm red line, engine coolant temperature, and supercharger boost. Also located on the dash panel were two power ports and a pair of small cupholders.

Standard equipment included AM/FM radio with cassette, Power Equipment Group (dual electric remote control mirrors, power side windows, power door locks), manual control air conditioning, speed control, dark tint sliding rear window, floor mats, and remote keyless illuminated entry system.

Ford kept its original promise that the Lightning would go on sale for less than $30,000. It was a close call with the Lightning's manufacturer's suggested retail price (MSRP) coming in at $29,995, including a $640 destination and delivery cost. Only three options were offered for the Lightning; a tonneau ($200), a premium electronic AM/FM stereo cassette, 6-disc CD changer ($210), and the Class III Trailer Towing Group ($245).

F-150 model and option prices (1999)

Model	MSRP*
Styleside 4x2 Regular Cab	
120in wb, Work Series	$15,250
120in wb, XL	$16,220
120in wb, XLT	$19,065
120in wb, Lariat	$22,425
139in wb, Work Series	$15,540
139in wb, XL	$16,520
139in wb, XLT	$19,360
139in wb, Lariat	$22,725
Flareside 4x2 Regular Cab	
120in wb, XL	$17,230
1120in wb, XLT	$20,075
120in wb, Lariat	$23,435
Styleside 4x4 Regular Cab	
120in wb, Work Series	$18,470
120in wb, XL	$19,560
120in wb, XLT	$22,580
120in wb, Lariat	$26,125
139in wb, Work Series	$18,760
139in wb, XL	$19,860
139in wb, XLT	$22,885
139in wb, Lariat	$26,425
Flareside 4x4 Regular Cab	
120in wb, XL	$20,570
120in wb, XLT	$23,590
120in wb, Lariat	$27,135
Styleside 4x2 SuperCab	
139in wb, Work Series	$17,840
139in wb, XL	$18,905
139in wb, XLT	$21,800
139in wb, Lariat	$25,165
157in wb, Work Series	$18,130
157in wb, XL	$19,205
157in wb, XLT	$22,100
157in wb, Lariat	$25,465
Flareside 4x2 SuperCab	
139in wb, XL	$19,915
139in wb, XLT	$22,810
139in wb, Lariat	$26,175
Styleside 4x4 SuperCab	
139in wb, Work Series	$21,570
139in wb, XL	$22,770
139in wb, XLT	$25,565
139in wb, Lariat	$28,555
157in wb, Work Series	$21,860
157in wb, XL	$23,070
157in wb, XLT	$26,065
157in wb, Lariat	$28,855
Flareside 4x4 SuperCab	
139in wb, XL	$23,780
139in wb, XLT	$26,775
139in wb, Lariat	$29,565

*Destination and Delivery charge was an additional $640.

continued next page

Options	Price
Engine	
4.6 liter V-8	$750
5.4 liter V-8 (Lariat and SuperCab)	$665
All others	$1415
5.4 liter Bi-Fuel Prep. System	
Lariat (Reg. Cab only)	$815
All others (Reg. Cab only)	$1565
Electronic Automatic Overdrive Trans.	$995
Limited slip rear axle	$285
Optional axle ratio Upgrade	$50
Limited slip with Optional axle ratio Upgrade	$335
Payload Packages	
Payload Package #2-Work Series	$470
Payload Package #2-XL	$270
Payload package #2-XLT	$270
Payload Package #3-Work Series	$470
Payload Package #3-XL	$270
Payload Package #3-XLT	$270
Payload Package #3-Lariat	$270
Tires (depending on size and model)	$125-$695
Seats	
XL	
40/60 Split Bench	$260
XLT	
Captain's Chairs with console	$490
Lariat	
Leather Captain's Chairs with console	$490
Four-wheel ABS/4-Wheel Disc Brakes	$375
4x4 Off-Road Equipment Group	
Lariat	$785
XLT	$1145
Air Conditioning	$805
Cab steps, Regular Cab, 4x2 Styleside	$250
Cab steps, SuperCab, 4x2 Styleside	$300
Cab Steps, Tubular, Reg. Cab 4x4 SS and Flareside	$350
Cab Steps, Tubular, SuperCab 4x4 SS and Flareside	$400
Carpet Delete	
Lariat trim (includes floor mats delete)	(-$100)
XLT trim	(-$50)
Floor carpeting with XLT trim	$100
Convenience Group (XL only)	$345
Electric shift-on-the-fly 4x4	
(XL & Lariat only)	$150
Heavy-Duty Electrical/Cooling Package	$210
Reg. Cab carpeted floor mats XL/XLT)	$30
SuperCab front and rear carpeted floor mats (XL/XLT)	$50
Fog Lamps (4x4 only)	$140
Fuel System Natural Gas (Bi-Fuel)	$5810
Fuel System Propane (Bi-Fuel)	$4950
Fuel System In-Bed Dual w/66N (Bi-Fuel)	$1280
Fuel System In-Bed Dual w/66P (Bi-Fuel)	$135
Engine Black Heater	$90
NASCAR Package	$150
Lower two-tone paint (XL/XLT/Lariat only)	$225
Power Driver's Seat/Autolamp (XLT only)	$360
Remote Keyless Entry/Anti-Theft (XLT only)	$150
Skid Plates (Reg. Cab SWB 4x4)	$80

continued over

Model year Lightning production was limited to 4000 units of which 1601 were painted black, 1543 were red, and 866 were white.

Charles Shortridge's claim that the Lightning could accelerate from zero to 60mph in less than seven seconds was easily supported by independent road test results. For example, *Car and Driver* (January 1999) reported these acceleration times:

0-30mph	2.2sec
0-40mph	3.1sec
0-50mph	4.3sec
0-60mph	5.8sec
0-70mph	7.4sec
0-80mph	9.4sec
0-90mph	12.0sec
0-100mph	15.2sec
Top Speed	139mph
Standing-start ¼mile:	14.4sec@97mph

The content of the F-150's three trim levels was revised for the 2000 model year. F-150's with the XL Sport Group had a color-keyed egg crate grille and surround. The bumpers and the caps of the manually-controlled mirrors were also color-keyed. P255/70RRXC16 All-Season OWL tires were standard for 4x2 models. All-Terrain versions were optional for 4x4 models. Replacing Ford's light-duty, under 8500lb GVW F-250 was a new F-150 7700lb Payload Group. It retained the F-250's heavier frame, larger brakes, higher-capacity 7-lug, 16in wheels, LT245 tires (4x2: All-Season; 4x4: All-Terrain), heavy-duty shocks and springs, Heavy Duty Electrical/Cooling Group, auxiliary transmission oil cooler and 8800 pound towing capacity. It also included a 3.73 axle ratio. This option was available

Options	Price
Skid Plates (all other 4x4 models)	$160
Snow Plow Prep Package (LWB Reg. Cab 4x4 only)	$505
Speed Control/Tilt Steering Wheel	$495
Sport Group XL 4x2	$495
Sport Group XL 4x4	$595
Sport Group XLT 4x2	$595
Sport Group XLT 4x4	$595
Front Tow Hooks (4x4 only)	$40
Class III Trailer Towing Group	$400
Aluminum Wheels (XL)	$200
Sliding Rear Window	$125
Tonneau Cover	$150
Electronic AM/FM Stereo/Clock/Cassette (XL)	$130
Electronic AM/FM Stereo/Clock/Single CD Player (XL)	$320
Electronic AM/FM Stereo/Clock/Single CD Player (XLT)	$190
CD Changer, 6-disc w/AM/FM Premium Stereo Cassette (XLT)	$400
CD Changer, 6-disc w/AM/FM Premium Stereo Cassette (Lariat)	$210
Daytime Running Lamps (Fleet only, Limited Production Option)	$45

This 17in cast aluminum wheel with chrome hub cover was optional for the 1999 XLT and standard for the Lariat. (Author's collection)

The 16in Argent painted steel wheel with Argent hub cover, which was standard for the 1999 Work Series trucks. (Author's collection)

This 16in polished aluminum wheel with a chrome hub cover was standard for the 1999 XLT. It was included with the Sport Group option for the XL. (Author's collection)

The 1999 XL's standard wheel was this 16in Argent painted steel wheel with an Argent hub cover. (Author's collection)

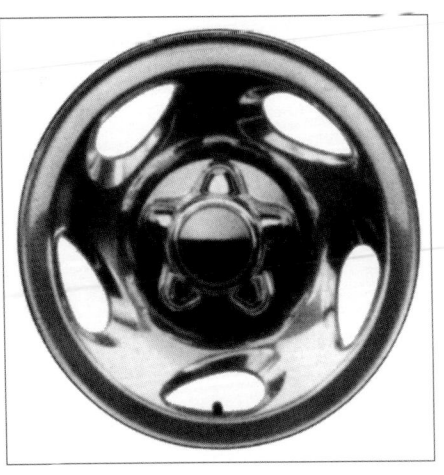

This 17in cast aluminum wheel with chrome hub cover was offered only as part of the Sport Group option for the XLT. (Author's collection)

A detailed view of the 2000 F-150's short- and long-arm independent front suspension. (Author's collection)

The horsepower of the 5.4 liter Triton V-8 was increased to 260, 25hp more than the 1998 engine. (Author's collection)

on 139in wheelbase 4x2/4x4 Styleside Regular Cab and SuperCab pickups powered by the 5.4 liter V-8. Both the 4x4, 139in wheelbase Super Cab and Regular Cab models equipped with this option and the Snow Plow Prep Group were recommended for snow plowing. Ford advised that on the 4x4 a front 4150lb GAWR was suitable for this purpose.

Aside from this development, which was essentially a nomenclature change, there were additional refinements throughout the F-150 line. A "comfort-enhancing" flip-up 40/60 rear seat with an improved 18-degree rear seat angle was adopted for the SuperCab. XLT and Lariat pickups (available only as a SuperCab), had new overhead consoles and passenger/driver visor vanity mirrors. Both were optional for the XL. A driver's side keypad entry system was now optional for the Lariat pickups. Chromed steel wheels with 17in OWL tires were standard.

All pickups had a new driver's side grab handle, positioned on the A-pillar. The instrument panel now included a redesigned cupholder/ash cup. Larger cupholders in the center console accompanied the Captain's Chair option.

All 4x2 models could be ordered with the chromed steel wheels and 17in OWL tires that were previously available only for 4x4 models. Placed on the rear fenders of all 4x4 pickups was a '4x4' decal. Tow hooks and a soft tonneau cover were added to the option list for 4x4 Work Series trucks. Due to low demand, the Rear Seat Delete option was dropped for the Work Series. Cab steps were now available on XL models.

Two new Clearcoat Metallic colors debuted in 2000; Island Blue and Chestnut. Colors no longer offered were: Dark Toreador Red and Teal. Two-tone paint schemes were now available on XLT Flareside and XLT with the Off-Road Group Pickups. Replacing Medium Prairie Tan as an interior color was Medium Parchment.

For improved fuel economy, pickup truck customers could now combine P235 tires with a 3.55:1 axle ratio. A 3.31 rear axle replaced the 3.55 unit as the standard ratio for many models. Still available were the F-150 natural gas, bi-fuel natural gas, and bi-fuel propane models.

On June 26, 2000, Ford announced the assembly of its 15,000th bi-fuel vehicle, a bi-fuel natural gas F-150. Ford built its bi-fuel propane (LPG) and natural gas trucks at its Oakville, Ontario plant. They were then shipped to GFI Control Systems in Cambridge, ON for installation of alternative fuel tanks and fuel systems. Ford's partnership with GFI began in 1994 with the bi-fuel natural gas F-150.

Due to low demand, the Carpet Delete option was no longer offered for the Lariats. The XLT received the same overhead console and visor vanity mirrors along with color-keyed carpeted floor mats with 'F-series'

The factory-installed soft tonneau cover was optional for XL, XLT, and Lariat models (Author's collection)

33

This bench seat was standard for both the Work Series and XL trucks for 1999. The Work Series was finished in vinyl and available in Medium Graphite or Medium Prairie Tan. The XL had cloth upholstery available in those colors as well as Dark Denim Blue and Dark Graphite, both new for 1999. (Author's collection)

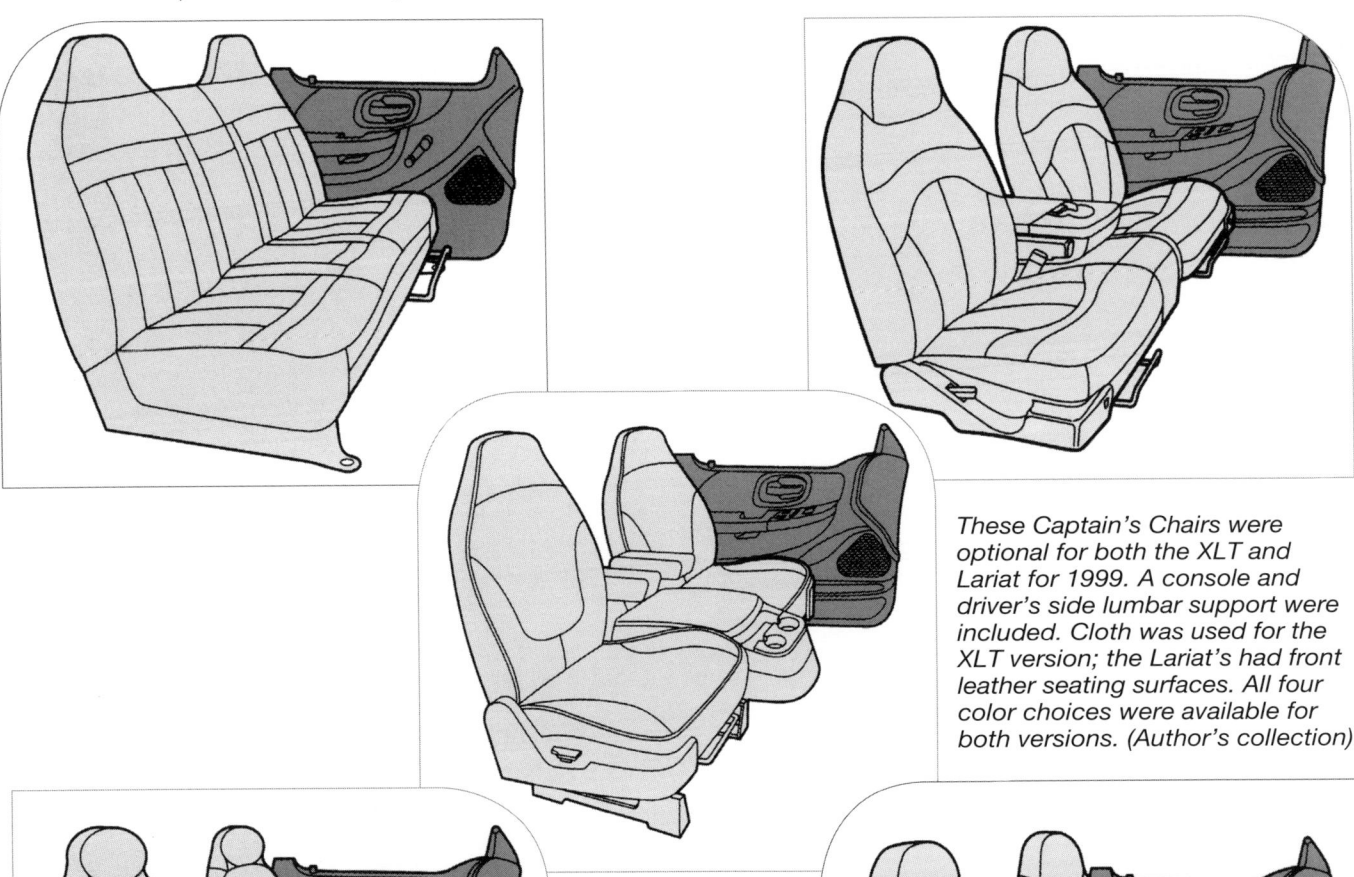

The standard 40/60 bench seat for the 1999 XLT was equipped with recliners, armrest, and a driver's side manual lumbar support. It was available in the same colors as the XL seat. It was also an option for the XL. (Author's collection)

These Captain's Chairs were optional for both the XLT and Lariat for 1999. A console and driver's side lumbar support were included. Cloth was used for the XLT version; the Lariat's had front leather seating surfaces. All four color choices were available for both versions. (Author's collection)

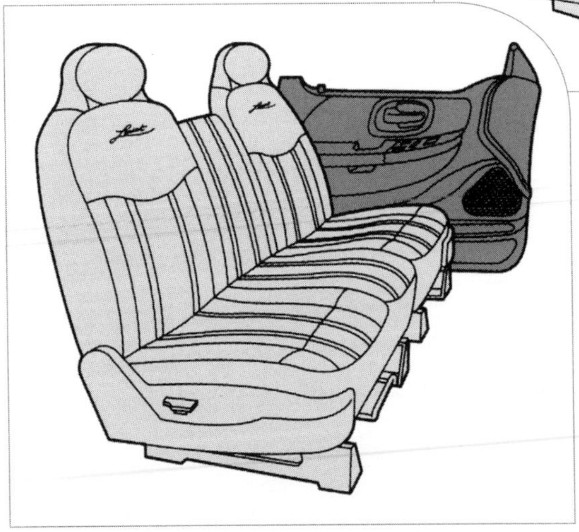

The standard 1999 Lariat seat was this split bench with front leather seating surfaces with vinyl in the rear of SuperCabs. All color choices were offered. (Author's collection)

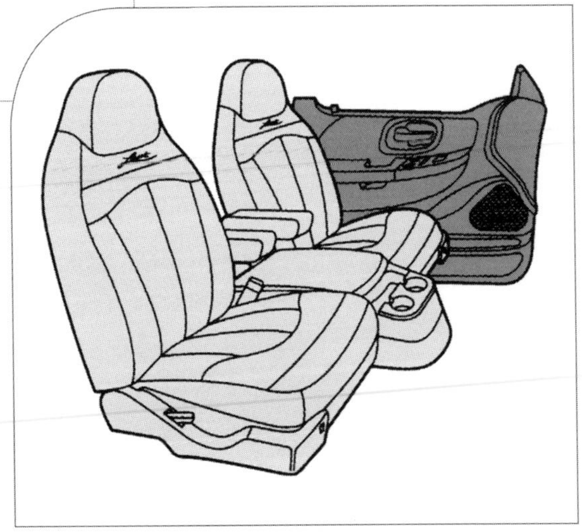

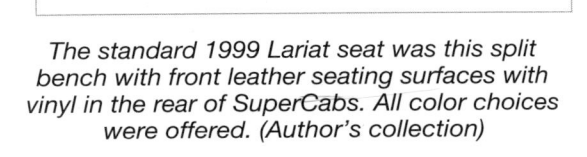

These Captain's Chairs with front leather seating areas were optional for the Lariat. Medium Graphite and Medium Prairie Tan were the color choices. (Author's collection)

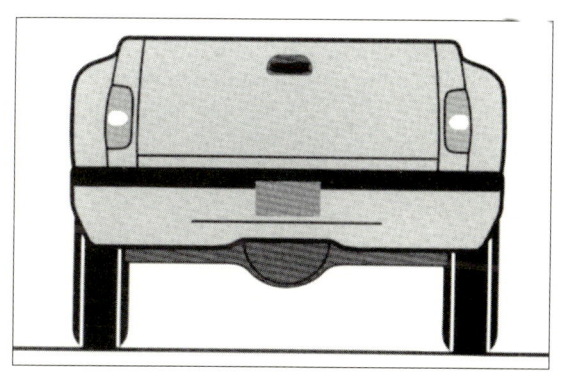

The major distinctions between the Styleside and Flareside pickup boxes of the 2000 F-150 are evident in this view. (Author's collection)

A 2000 F-150 XLT 4x4 Styleside Pickup. (Courtesy of Ford Media Services)

monograms. Both the XL and Work series models now had a standard cargo light.

The content of many option packages was restructured. Added to the XL Convenience Group was the previously described overhead console. This option still included speed control/tilt steering wheel and a tailgate lock.

No longer offered was the Pickup Box Security Group option. Its content was now incorporated into the XL Convenience Group.

F-150's ordered with the Off-Road Group and the 5.4 liter engine had the 3.55 axle ratio. In 1999 the ratio had been 3.73. Ford reported that this change did not result in any performance loss, while providing better fuel economy. In the 55R Off-Road Group, 17in cast aluminum 5-lug wheels replaced the chromed steel wheels. A steel wheel was used for the spare. Lariat pickups with this option now carried a '4x4 Off-Road' decal. To appeal to what Ford depicted as "value-conscious customers", the OWL tires of the 1999 version of the 622/623 Payload Groups were replaced with black side wall tires. OWL tires were optional only on the XLT.

On February 15, 2000 the F-150 2WD pickup powered by the 4.2 liter V-6 became a "Greener Choice", by virtue of being the only full-size pickup cited in the American Council for an Energy Efficient Economy's Green Book listing of environmentally friendly vehicles. This annual report was compiled by using a formula considering the number of vehicle's produced, their total life cycle emissions, and the type of fuel used. Earlier, F-150's with this engine were certified as Low Emission Vehicles (LEV) since they emitted no more than half the smog-forming emissions of other vehicles.

Both developments were welcomed by Ford executives. Helen Ptrauskas, Ford vice-president for Environmental and Safety Engineering said, "We're very pleased and proud

A 2000 F-150 XLT SuperCab Flareside. (Courtesy of Ford Media Services)

35

The six basic configurations offered for the 2000 F-150. (Author's collection).

Regular Cab SWB
Styleside
119.9" WB 4x2
120.2" WB 4x4

Regular Cab SWB
Flareside
119.9" WB 4x2
120.2" WB 4x4

Regular Cab LWB
Styleside
138.5" WB 4x2
138.8" WB 4x4

SuperCab SWB
Styleside
138.5" WB 4x2
138.8" WB 4x4

SuperCab SWB
Flareside
138.5" WB 4x2
138.8" WB 4x4

SuperCab LWB
Styleside
157.1" WB 4x2
157.4" WB 4x4

that the positive environmental benefits of the F-150 have been recognized. It's the bestselling vehicle in the United States, so the positive benefit is significant." Referring to Ford's year-earlier pledge that all F-series pickups, sport utilities, and mini vans would met LEV standards, Ford's vice president, North American Truck, Gurminder Bedi, added that, "It's just the right thing to do, and part of Ford's 'Cleaner, Safer, Sooner' strategy for trucks."

Ford had no qualms in acknowledging that the 2000 F-150 was "essentially a carryover from the 1999 model year with minor exterior and interior improvements". But there was nothing carryover or minor about the limited edition Harley-Davidson F-150 pickup.

Its debut had been widely anticipated by both trucking and biking enthusiasts since earlier, at Bike Week, 1999 in Daytona Beach, Florida, Ford and Harley-Davidson had announced a five-year alliance. As the first co-branded product of Ford and Harley-Davidson, it united two of the most recognized icons of American transportation culture that would be celebrating their centennials in 2003.

The new model was introduced on August 9, 1999 at the Sturgis, South Dakota Annual Rally & Races. This was regarded as the premier motorcycle event in the US, attracting 350,000 motorcyclists from around the world. Dubbed the 'Born in Detroit, Dressed in Milwaukee' truck, the latest F-150 was equipped with cast chromed aluminum, vented five-spoke wheels measuring 20x9in, making it the first Ford production vehicle to be

36

The 2000 F-150 Work Series standard 16 x7in, 5-lug Argent painted steel wheel with Argent hub cover. (Author's collection)

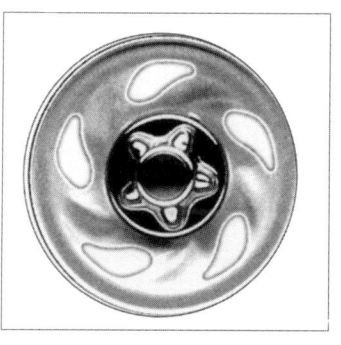

Standard for the 2000 XL F-150, and optional for the Work Series with Payload Group options for the V-6 and V-8 engines, was this 16 x7in, 5-lug Argent styled steel wheel with a chrome hub cover. (Author's collection)

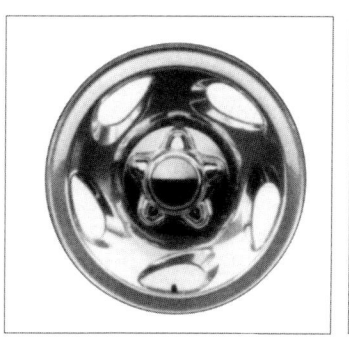

This 16 x 7in 5-lug polished aluminum wheel with a chrome hub cover was standard for the 2000 XLT, and included in the optional XL Sport Group. (Author's collection)

Optional only for the 2000 XLT was this 16 x 7in 5-lug, 5-spoke cast aluminum wheel with a chrome hub cover. (Author's collection)

equipped with 20in wheels. They were custom made for Ford by Superior Industries International, Inc. in Van Nuys, California and were also fitted with a brushed-on polished Harley-Davidson logo center cap. These wheels and the truck's G2 275/45 R20 Goodyear Eagle GT II tires were among styling cues linking it with the Harley-Davidson mystique. "This 'Built Ford Tough' truck", said George Magro, Ford's project manager of the Ford/Harley-Davidson Alliance, "will have a lot of wheel, a lot of tire, and a lot of attitude.

"We worked with Harley-Davidson to design features that would be distinctive, not distracting", explained Magro, "the wheel is one of the strongest statements on the truck." Other Ford and Harley-Davidson executives were equally enthusiastic about this new example of "American Muscle".

"The Harley-Davidson F-150 is an exciting truck that has power and presence, symbolizing the 'Authentic American Muscle' tradition of both companies", said Gurminder Bedi. "Many Harley owners also own Ford trucks", he added. "We believe they'll want to park this truck next to their prized Harley-Davidson motorcycle."

Concurring was Harley-Davidson's chairman and chief executive officer, Jeff Bluestein, who joined Bedi in unveiling the new truck:

"This alliance brings together two of the most well-known and admired companies in the world. Ford and Harley-Davidson customers alike want a distinctive vehicle that makes a statement about themselves as individuals." Later in the year, George Magro announced that Ford would sponsor the annual 'Love Ride 16' in Glendale, California, which was one of the world's largest single day charity fund raisers as well as one of the largest motorcycle events held California. Love Ride 16 was a 50 mile motorcycle ride whose proceeds went to the *Los Angeles Times'* Reading By 9 program and the Muscular Dystrophy Association, which was the official charity of Harley-Davidson. "This is a great event for wonderful causes", Magro said, "and the Love Ride is a great place to introduce the

The 2000 XLT F-150 interior with standard 40/60 bench seat. (Courtesy of Ford Media Services)

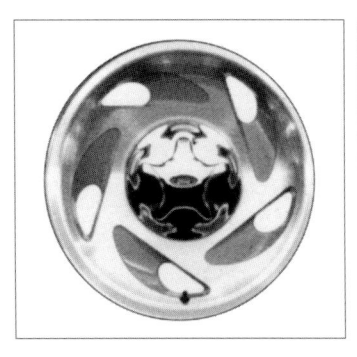

This 17 x 7.5in cast aluminum wheel with chrome hub cover was available only with 4x4 Off-Road Equipment for XLT and Lariats, and the XLT Sport Group. (Author's collection)

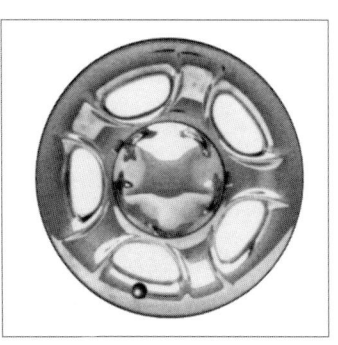

Standard for the 2000 F-150 Lariat was this 17 x 7.5in chrome steel wheel with chrome hub cover. (Author's collection)

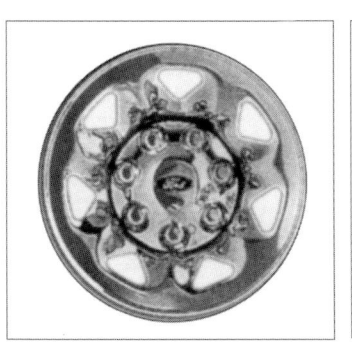

This 7-lug 16 x 7.0in Argent styled steel wheel with an Argent hub cover was included and available only with the 7700 Payload Group option for the Work Series and XL models. (Author's collection)

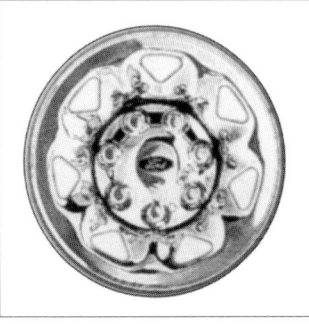

This 7-lug 16 x 7.0in Chrome styled steel wheel with chrome hub cover was included and available only in the 7700 Payload Group option for the XL, XLT, and Lariat. (Author's collection)

new Harley-Davidson to Southern California enthusiasts". For its part, Ford donated a Harley-Davidson F-150 as a grand prize of the Love Ride.

The Harley-Davidson F-150 began as a 4x2 SuperCab on a 139in wheelbase fitted with a Flareside box. A hard shell tonneau was standard as was a 5.4 liter Triton V-8 with 260hp and 350lb/ft of torque, and a 4-speed automatic transmission. A 3.73:1 axle ratio was specified. Providing an appropriate exhaust tone was a sport-tuned single inlet SVT Lightning muffler ending in dual chrome 3.5in round 'slash cut' tips. Ford reported that "design engineers ... specially tuned the single-inlet-dual-outlet exhaust to give it a more 'robust' aural signature".

The suspension was lowered by one inch and used revised springs and sway bar.

A black finish with a Gray and Harley-Davidson Orange accent stripe was the only exterior color offered. This was virtually a 100 per cent monochromatic theme with the front and rear bumpers, tonneau cover, and grille surround all finished in the black body color. Both the pickup box side rails and tailgate top caps were finished in black. The front lower valance included driving lamps and a black, quasi-billet insert. Chrome was used for the grille and the truck's nurf bars. Unified Ford/Harley-Davidson badges were positioned on the front fenders. Contained in the windshield was a Harley-Davidson bar and shield dot pattern and Alliance logo.

The truck's "mainly black with just a dash of chrome" theme was maintained by its interior. Ebony black nudo leather Captain's Chairs carried Tyca Harley-Davidson logos on their seat backs. A black leather accessory pouch was located on the center console, the four-spoke steering wheel had a jeweled air bag cover and was covered in black leather. A Harley-Davidson "spun metal" instrument cluster was used. The front door inserts and armrests were finished in black leather trim. Contrasting with

F-150 accessories

Air conditioning
Airbag lock
Bed mat
Cargo net
Compass mirror
Engine block heater
Hood deflector
Interior cargo liner
Locking gas cap
Molded splash guards
Pickup box rails
Rally bars
Rear Step Bumper
Removable trailer-tow mirror
Seven-pin wiring system
Soft tonneau cover
Speed control
Step/sill plates
Tailgate protector
Tool box
Truck cover

Air filtration system
Bed hooks/tie down
Bike Carriers
Class III trailer hitch
Daytime running lights
Floor mats
Integral fog lights
Leather-wrapped steering wheel
Manual sliding rear window
Pickup box front end protector
Power sliding rear window
Rapid heat storage system
Remote keyless entry system
Running boards
Side window deflector
Spare tire lock
Sport hood cover
Styled wheel protector lock
Tire step
Trailer hitch balls
Wood trim (dash and door switch plates)

1. Instrument panel dimmer switch
2. Headlamp control
3. Instrument cluster
4. Speed control(1)
5. Automatic transmission gearshift lever with overdrive lockout switch(1)
6. Audio system controls
7. Passenger airbag deactivation switch
8. Climate controls
9. 4WD control(1)
10. Auxiliary power point
11. Driver airbag
12. Turn signal, washer control and high-beam switch

(1) If equipped.

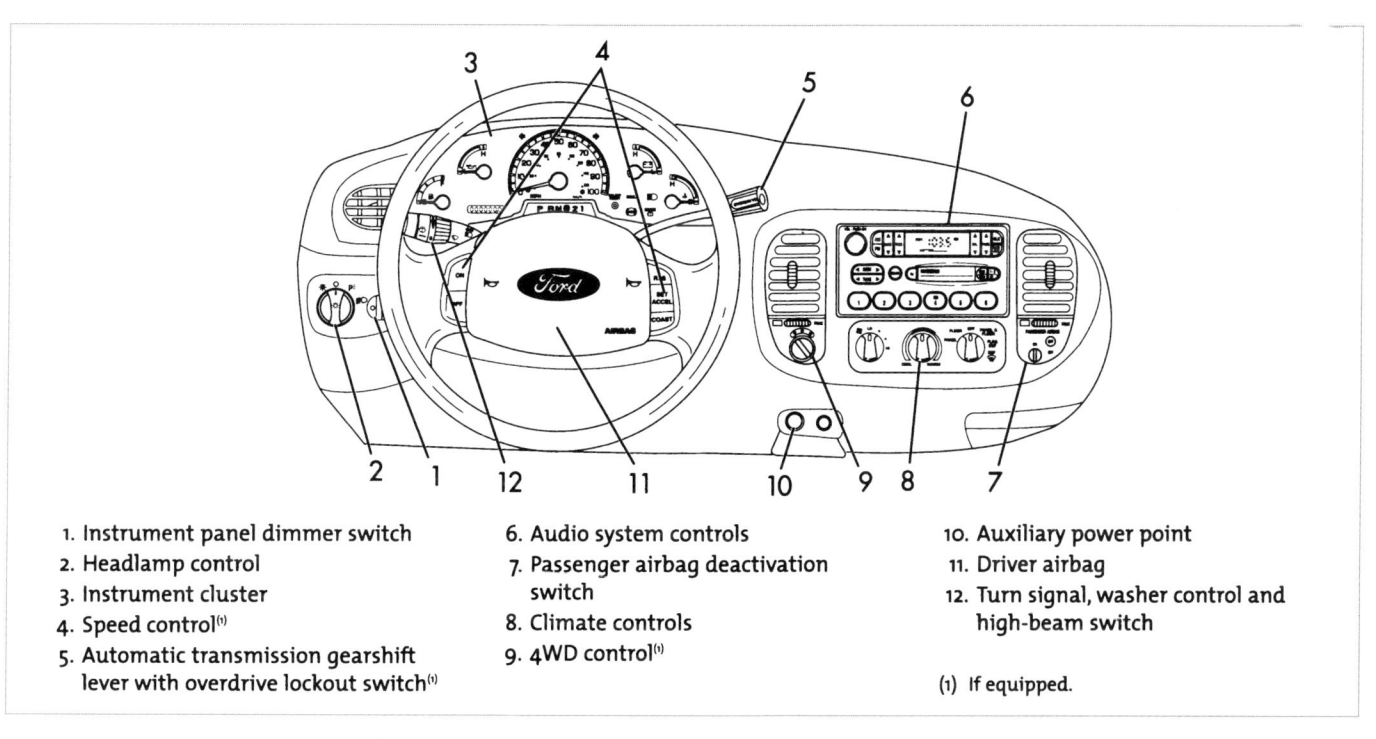

The 2000 F-150 instrument panel. (Author's collection)

this trim were chrome steering column stalks, door releases, and seat levers.

Rounding out the truck's standard equipment was air conditioning, speed control, tilt steering wheel, keyless entry, power windows/locks/driver's seat, overhead console with temperature and compass, privacy glass, and AM/FM stereo with single CD player.

Upon its introduction, Ford set the MSRP of the Harley-Davidson F-150 at $32,995. Ford also announced that three options would be available; 6-disc CD changer ($400), sliding rear window ($125), and engine block heater ($90).

The only facility selected to produce the Harley-Davidson F-150 was Ford's Ontario Truck Plant in Oakville, Ontario. Job #1 (production start up) was scheduled for April 10, 1999, with the first examples appearing in dealer showrooms in the spring of 2000. Obviously pleased that the H-D F-150 was joining the Lightning as the second limited edition F-series pickup to be produced at Oakville, was Bobbie Gaunt, Ford of Canada's president and CEO. At a special ceremony where the Harley-Davidson F-150 complete, reported Ford, "with throaty growl", joined other trucks assembled at the Ontario plant, including the Super-Duty, Crew Cab, and SVT Lightning. Gaunt said, "The decision to give OPT exclusive manufacturing privileges for this special-edition F-series is high praise for the men and women who build them, and whose commitment to quality is second to none."

Plant manager Patricia Reid also spoke highly of the work ethic of the Ford employees at Ontario. "OPT people have an impressive track record in assembling dramatically different niche vehicles that roll down the same line as the rest of the F-series models they build", she said. "Most importantly, our employees combine excellent productivity with top quality."

For his part, Brant Noltie, Ford of Canada's Truck Group brand manager, placed the production of the new Ford truck in the perspective of the F-150's enduring popularity in Canada. "Ford's F-series have been the top-selling pickups in Canada for an astonishing 34 consecutive years, and the best selling vehicle for six years", he said. "This truck fuses the 'Built Ford Tough' durability of the F-150 with the almost mythic popularity and appeal of the Harley-Davidson brand name."

The new Ford quickly proved to be very popular, with Jay Leno becoming customer number one. Anyone else wanting a new Harley-Davidson F-150 had to act quickly since the entire 8000 unit production run had been ordered by Ford dealers within five days. It almost immediately became an icon for both bikers and truckers.

Several detail changes identified the latest Lightning model from the debut version. Along with those on all F-150s, the inserts of the Lightning's exterior mirrors were now colored. The rear window glass was tinted and the backup clear lenses were moved from the middle to the top of the tail lamp unit. Since the Lightning was based on the XLT, it was fitted with the new overhead console with compass, outside air temperature, and storage.

In addition to the many factory-installed options offered for the F-150 were numerous accessories available from Ford dealers.

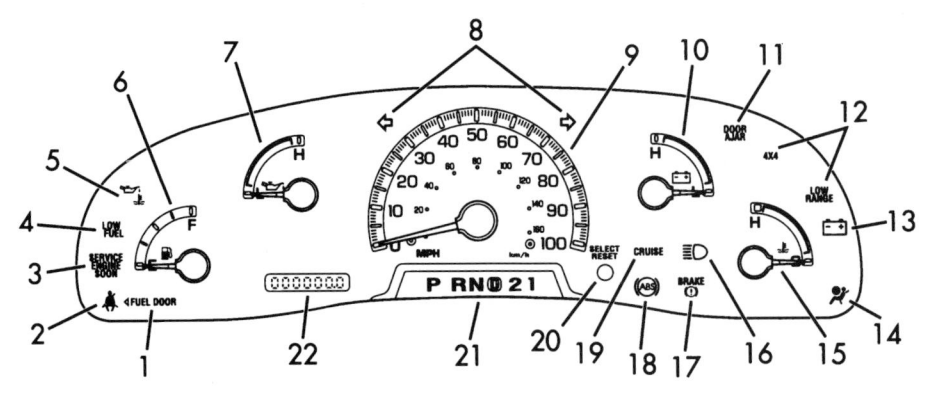

1. Fuel door location reminder
2. Fasten safety belt warning light
3. Service engine soon warning light
4. Low fuel warning light
5. Oil pressure/engine coolant temperature warning light
6. Fuel gauge
7. Engine oil pressure gauge
8. Turn signal indicators
9. Speedometer
10. Voltmeter
11. Door ajar warning light
12. 4x4 system indicator lights[1]
13. Charging system warning light
14. Airbag readiness indicator/ warning light
15. Engine coolant temperature gauge
16. High-beam indicator light
17. Brake system warning light/ parking brake
18. Anti-lock Braking System warning light
19. Speed control indicator light
20. Trip odometer select/reset button
21. Automatic transmission gearshift indicator[1]
22. Odometer/trip odometer

(1) If equipped.

Details of the 2000 F-150 instrument cluster. (Author's collection)

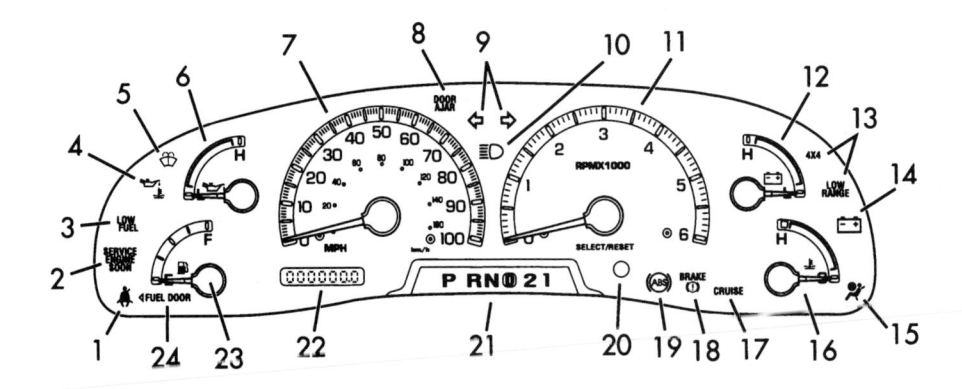

1. Fasten safety belt warning light
2. Service engine soon warning light
3. Low fuel warning light
4. Oil pressure/engine coolant temperature warning light
5. Low windshield washer fluid light
6. Engine oil pressure gauge
7. Speedometer
8. Door ajar warning light
9. Turn signal indicators
10. High-beam indicator light
11. Tachometer
12. Voltmeter
13. 4x4 system indicator lights[1]
14. Charging system warning light
15. Airbag readiness indicator/ warning light
16. Engine coolant temperature gauge
17. Speed control indicator light
18. Brake system warning light/ parking brake
19. Anti-lock Braking System warning light
20. Trip odometer/select/reset button
21. Automatic transmission gearshift indicator[1]
22. Odometer/trip odometer
23. Fuel gauge
24. Fuel door location reminder

(1) If equipped.

A comparison of the 2000 F-150 tachometer cluster option with the 1999 version shows the variations that exist between the two types. (Author's collection)

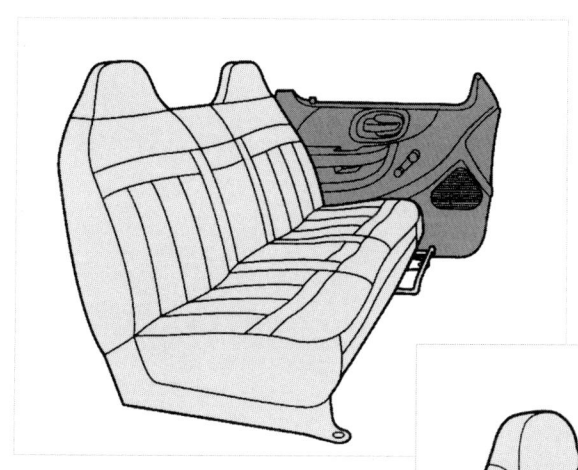

The standard bench seat for the 2000 F-150 Work Series. It had a vinyl finish available in either Dark Denim Blue, or Medium Graphite. With cloth upholstery it was standard for the XL in Medium Graphite, Medium Parchment or Dark Graphite, and optional in Dark Denim Blue or Medium Graphite for the Work Series. The vinyl version, in Medium Graphite only, was also optional for the XL. (Author's collection)

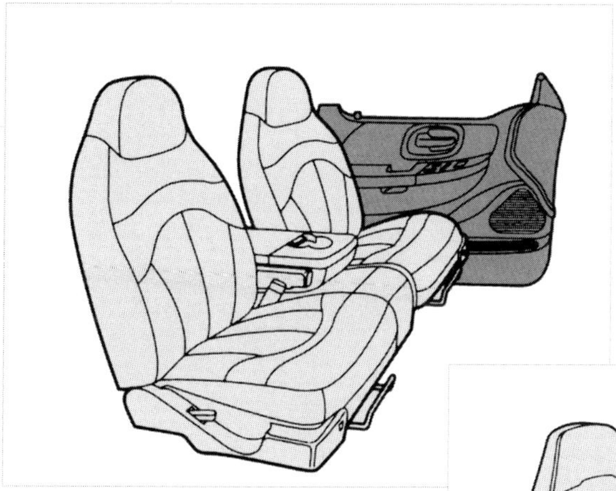

The 2000 F-150 XLT's standard seat was this cloth 40/60 Split Bench seat with driver's side lumbar support in Medium Graphite, Medium Parchment, or Dark Graphite. This seat was optional for the XL. (Author's collection)

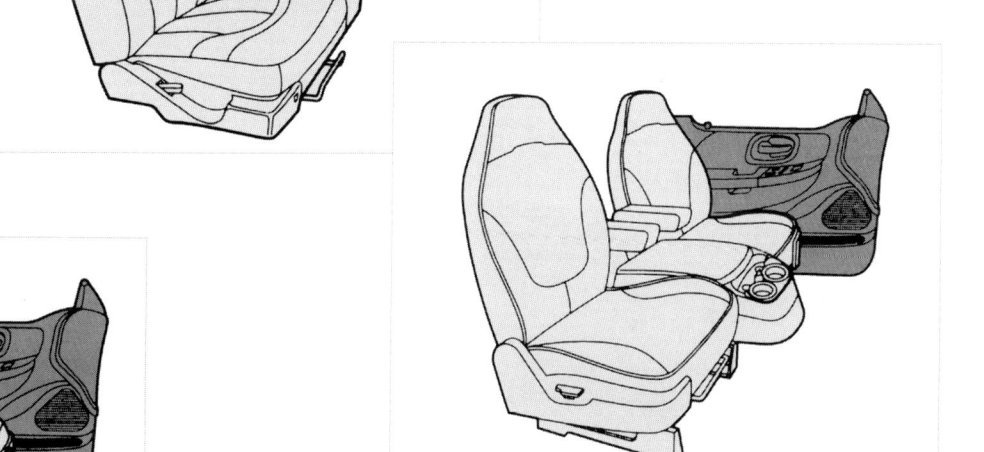

The 2000 XLT's optional cloth-covered Captain's Chairs with console and driver's lumbar was offered in Medium Graphite, Medium Parchment, or Dark Graphite. (Author's collection)

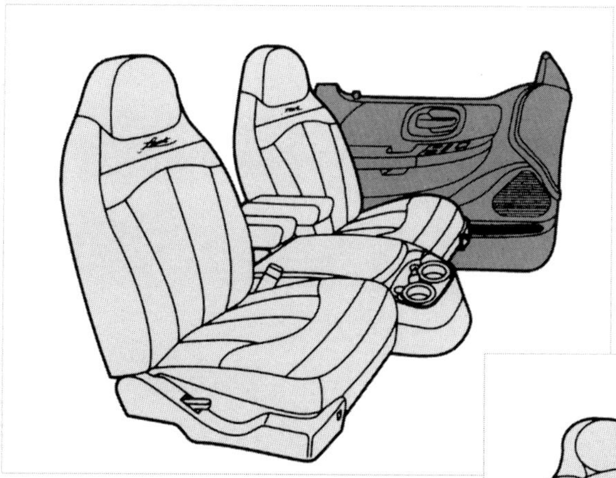

The 2000 Lariat's optional Captain's Chairs and console. It had front leather seating surfaces and was offered in Medium Graphite or Medium Parchment. (Author's collection)

The 2000 Lariat's standard 60/40 split bench seat. It had front leather seating areas and was available in Medium Graphite or Medium Parchment. (Author's collection)

41

A 2000 F-150 XLT Flareside. (Courtesy of Ford Media Services)

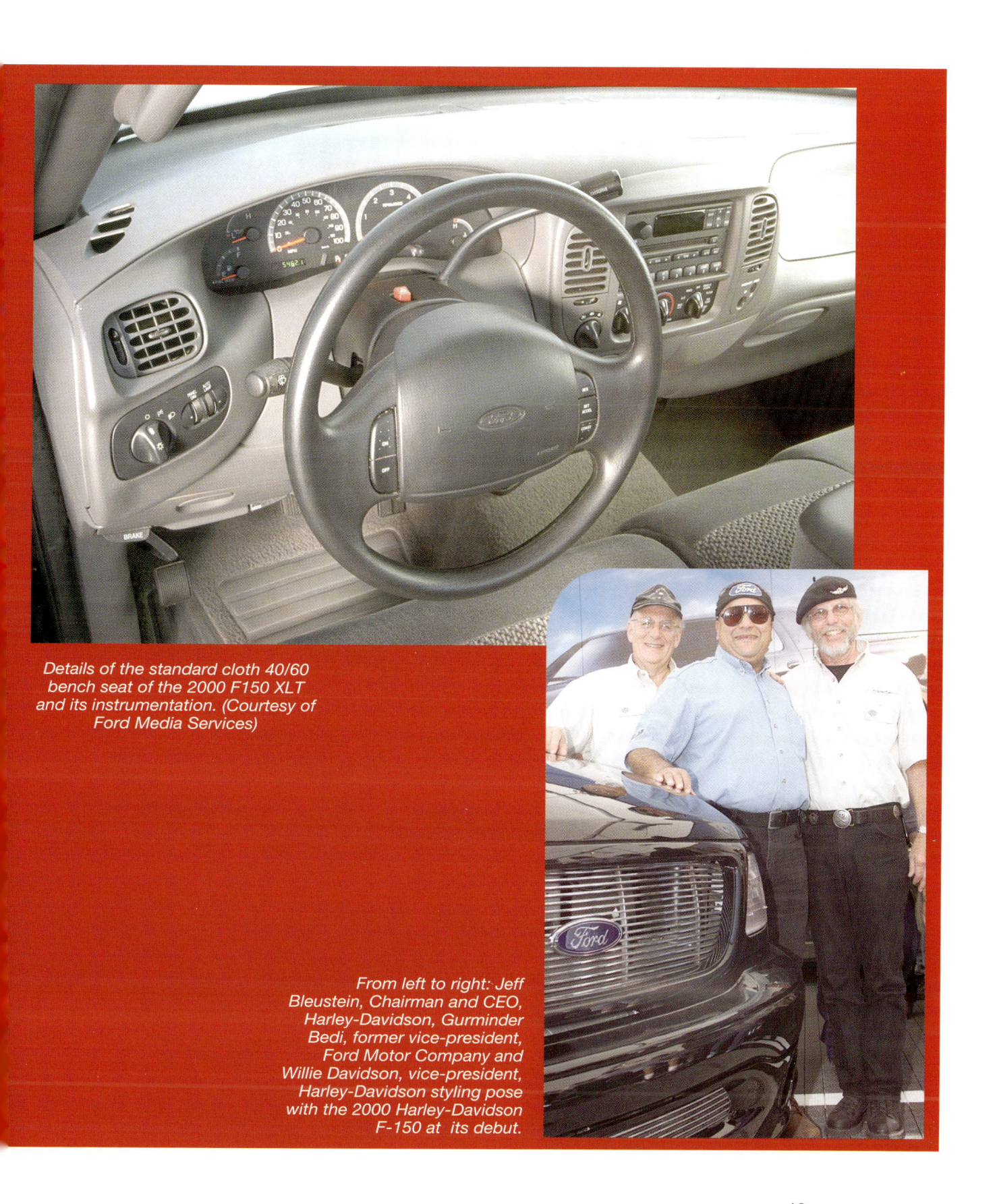

Details of the standard cloth 40/60 bench seat of the 2000 F150 XLT and its instrumentation. (Courtesy of Ford Media Services)

From left to right: Jeff Bleustein, Chairman and CEO, Harley-Davidson, Gurminder Bedi, former vice-president, Ford Motor Company and Willie Davidson, vice-president, Harley-Davidson styling pose with the 2000 Harley-Davidson F-150 at its debut.

Willie Davidson behind the wheel of the 2000 Harley-Davidson F-150 at Sturgis, South Dakota. Looking on are Gurminder Bedi and Jeff Bleustein. (Courtesy of Ford Media Services).

Below and top right: Two icons of the American road at rest and in motion. The 20-inch wheels of the 2000 Harley-Davidson Ford F-150 are shown to good advantage in these photographs. (Courtesy of Ford Media Services)

Another view of Jeff Bleustein, Gurminder Bedi and Willie Davidson with the 2000 Harley-Davidson Ford F-150 at its debut at Sturgis, South Dakota. (Courtesy of Ford Media Services)

Key aspects of the interior of the 2000 Harley-Davidson Ford F-150, its ebony black leather trimmed seats, embossed Harley-Davidson logo and black leather-wrapped steering wheel, are seen here. (Courtesy of Ford Media Services)

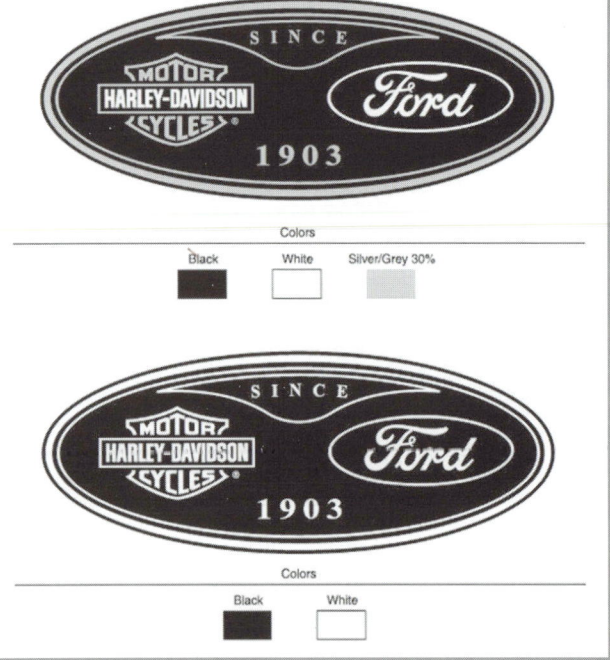

A close-up view of the Harley-Davidson Alliance logo which was incorporated in the windshield of the 2000 Harley-Davidson Ford F-150. (Courtesy of Ford Media Services).

The instrumentation of the 2000 F-150 Lightning used the F-150 tachometer cluster option. (Courtesy of Ford Media Services)

The 2000 Lightning's 20in wheels are prominent from this perspective. (Courtesy of Ford Media Services)

An evocative view of the Lightning leaving little to the imagination! (Courtesy of Ford Media Services)

The 2000 Lightning's tailgate carried both SVT and Ford badging. (Courtesy of Ford Media Services)

The 2000 F-150 Lightning in Bright Red Clearcoat. (Courtesy of Ford Media Services)

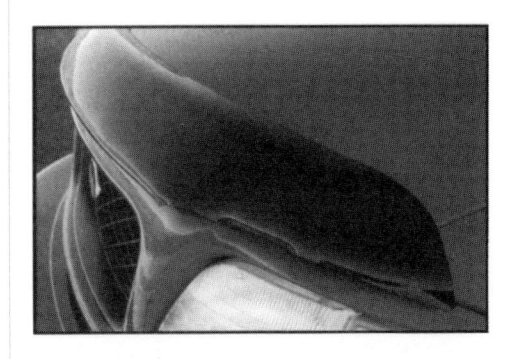

Wraparound Hood/Bug Deflector[1]

- A simple, effective way to help keep hood and windshield clean from airborne debris
- Wraparound design helps provide additional front-end protection and aerodynamic styling
- Specially designed vents help reduce wind resistance and allow proper distribution of windshield fluid
- Attaches easily and securely to underside of leading edge of hood

Front-end Cover

- Heavy-duty 22-oz. vinyl helps protect against chips and scratches caused by flying rocks, insects, salt and other road debris
- Custom fit for F-Series
- Available with vehicle name and/or Ford oval
- Unique design allows opening of hood without removing cover

Molded Running Boards[1]

- Add a customized, aerodynamic look with reduced step height
- Constructed of "TPO" plastic for added strength and durability
- Ribbed step pads offer added traction
- Available in all exterior colors
- Available for Regular Cab and SuperCab
- Dealer installation recommended

Bedliner[1]

- "The Gripper" skid-resistant surface, available for both under-the-rail and over-the-rail bedliners, helps reduce cargo shifting
- One-piece seamless construction fits securely against sidewalls
- Cargo-restraining system helps keep cargo securely in place
- Cam-lock fasteners allow for no-drill installation on over-the-rail bedliners
- Easy snap-in installation featured on under-the-rail bedliners

Four examples of the many accessories offered by Ford dealers for the 2000 F-150. (Author's collection)

3
2001-2003

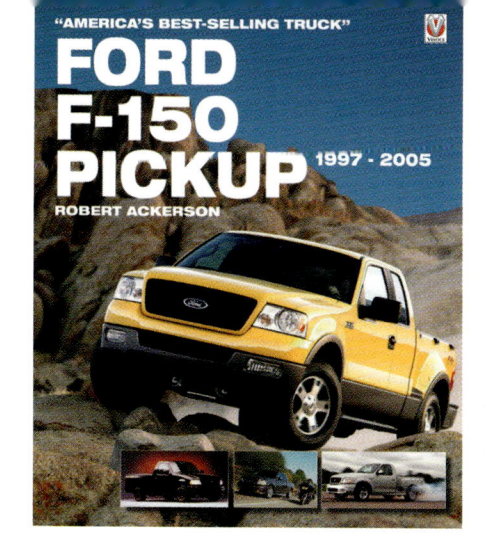

The 2001 F-150 SuperCrew was introduced at the Detroit Auto Shop in late 1999 by Ford Division President Jim O'Connor. (Courtesy of Ford Media Services)

The news from Ford, as it had been for so many years, was good when it introduced the 2001 F-150 trucks on August 31. "The Built Ford Tough F-series pickup," Ford Division Truck Group marketing manager Al Giombetti, announced, "has been the best-selling truck for 23 years, and has been the best-selling vehicle - car or truck - for the past 18 years."

The current 150 pickup platform was just past the midpoint of its production life, and annual model changes were mainly evolutionary in nature. Giombetti regarded this policy as one of the reasons for its popularity. "The only way to maintain that leadership, achieve those kinds of sales records and keep customers coming back", he explained, "is to evolve the product and deliver exactly what customers are looking for and have come to expect for a Ford truck."

Ford maintained the F-150 competitiveness with a steady infusion of new models. For 2001 the new model was the F-150 SuperCrew which was introduced as a 2001 model in the first quarter of 2000. The SuperCrew was the first truck with a GVW of under 8500lb with four full-sized doors and a full rear passenger configuration. In effect, the SuperCrew combined the features of two of Ford's most successful models; the comfort and interior space of the heavy-duty CrewCab with the versatility, ride, handling, and "garageability" of a light-duty SuperCab.

When Ford Division President, Jim O'Connor, presented the new model, he depicted it as "the ideal vehicle for business customers and growing families who need more interior space to go with the ruggedness and utility of a pickup".

The SuperCrew cab was one foot longer than the SuperCab's. Ford claimed this added length, along with its four conventional doors, gave the SuperCrew both best-in-class rear-seat roominess, and the easiest entry exit of all pickups available in the US. Whereas the SuperCab used smaller hinged doors that swung out from the C-pillar, the full-size SuperCrew doors were separated by a B-pillar on each side. Each door had interior and exterior handles. This was the same system as used on the Super Duty F-series CrewCab trucks.

A front 60/40 bench seat was standard, Captain's Chairs with a floor-mounted center console were optional. Ford also provided the SuperCrew with a fold-flat 60/40 rear seat similar to the one used in the Expedition SUV. An enclosed storage compartment made it possible to install an optional 6-disc CD player with a front bench seat. If the Captain's Chairs were ordered, this unit was mounted in the floor console. XLT and Lariat SuperCrews could also be ordered with a Rear Seat Entertainment System option. A premium AM/FM stereo radio with a single disc CD player was standard.

The 2001 F-150 SuperCrew was a response to dramatic changes in the US pickup truck market. In the mid-nineties, most Ford customers used their F-Series trucks primarily for work. By 2001, 70 per cent of customers were using them for personal use. At the same time many buyers of the SuperCab expressed an interest in an F-150 with similar towing and hauling capability, but with more room for six passengers. (Author's collection)

The SuperCrew was equipped with three child safety seat tethers, located in the back seat. The tether anchors provided an improved method for more securely buckling in child safety seats. Straps, available from many sources, were used to supplement the traditional safety belts for securing the child safety seats.

Power-adjustable pedals, a pickup truck first, were standard. The brake and accelerator pedals could be adjusted up to three inches rearward in a horizontal plane from their standard position. The SuperCrew pickup bed measured 5½ feet in length and was constructed with steel inner and composite outer panels. This bed size resulted in an overall length for the SuperCrew that was the same as a short wheelbase SuperCab. Ford claimed that it also gave the SuperCrew "better maneuverability and garageability than any other crew cab models".

SuperCrew major dimensions

Wheelbase	138.5in
Overall Length	225.9in (4x4: 226.2in)
Overall Width	79.1in (4x4: 79.9in)
Overall Height	73.9in (4x4: 76.9in)
Front Head Room	39.8in
Rear Head Room	39.8in
Front Leg Room	41.0in
Rear leg Room	36.8in
Front Shoulder Room	63.7in
Rear Shoulder Room	63.6in
Front Hip Room	59.8in
Rear Hip Room	58.0in

Ford conducted extensive customer research to determine the public's reaction to this new configuration. "The response", it reported, "from work and personal use customers was overwhelming. Customers said they truly appreciated the extra interior space, not only for people but for clean, dry, and secure storage for things such as tools and groceries".

"As a result", said Al Giombotti, Ford Truck Group manager, "offering a more user friendly, comfortable interior while maintaining pickup versatility is a swift answer to a new customer demand. We've seen the steady growth in the pickup truck

The 2001 Lariat F-150 SuperCrew. According to Ford, "One look at the exterior and you know this is a new 'Built-Ford Tough' F-150 truck." (Courtesy of Ford Media Services)

market for several years, lead in part by the personal use area."

The SuperCrew box had the same width at the wheel houses as other F-150s. Cargo capacity totaled 44.2 cubic feet. Standard payload was 1765lb, the same as the F-150 SuperCab. To accommodate its extra passenger capacity the SuperCrew was fitted with new body mounts and staggered rear shock absorbers.

After the SuperCrew was launched, Ford offered a bed extender which increased box length to seven feet, improving its usefulness. When the tailgate was closed, the stowed bed extender functioned as a storage area, keeping smaller items from sliding around the bed when the truck was in motion.

SuperCrew 4x4s could be ordered with the Off-Road Equipment Group. All models had standard four-wheel anti-lock braking and Ford's SecuriLock passive anti-theft system.

Initially, the SuperCrew's standard engine was Ford's 4.6 liter Triton V-6, developing 220hp@4500rpm and 290lb/ft of torque @3250rpm. When the complete F-150 line for 2001 was introduced, it was re-engineered from the block up for refined noise, vibration, and harshness (NVH) and identified as the Power Improved 4.6 liter Triton. Its improvements included a more robust ribbing pattern, thicker side-skirt walls, and redesigned air intake resonator and engine cover. Noise-reducing new materials were used for the engine cover and oil pan. it was rated at 231hp@4750rpm and 293lb/ft of torque @3500rpm. On December 11, 2001 *Ward's Auto World* named this engine to its "Ten Best" engine list for the sixth straight year. The optional 5.4 liter Triton rated at 260hp@4500rpm and 350lb/ft of torque @2500rpm and the 380hp supercharged version used in the SVT Lightning were included in this recognition. The 4.6 and 5.4 liter Triton engines met Federal Low Emission Vehicle (LEV) standards.

Ford offered the SuperCrew in XLT and Lariat trim levels. Both contained rear seat reading lamps, cupholders, and door map pockets, rear child-seat tethers, a rear seat power point, power-adjustable brake and accelerator pedals, privacy glass for the rear door and backlight, four-wheel anti-lock brakes, air conditioning, and power windows and locks.

The standard front overhead console included a compass, outside air-temperature gauge, and storage areas. 16in polished aluminum wheels and All-Season OWL P255 tires were standard on 4x2 and 4x4 models. XLT's were available with optional five-spoke 16in cast aluminum wheels. All-new 17in ten-spoke cast aluminum wheels were optional for the 4x4 XLT. Electronic shift on the fly was standard on 4x4 models, with skid plates optional.

The Lariat had standard 17in chromed steel wheels and OWL tires, with All-Season tires on 4x2 models, and All-Terrain on 4x4 models. A driver's door keyless-entry keypad was also standard. The Lariat interior had premium leather on the front and rear seating surfaces.

A power glass moon roof with an

53

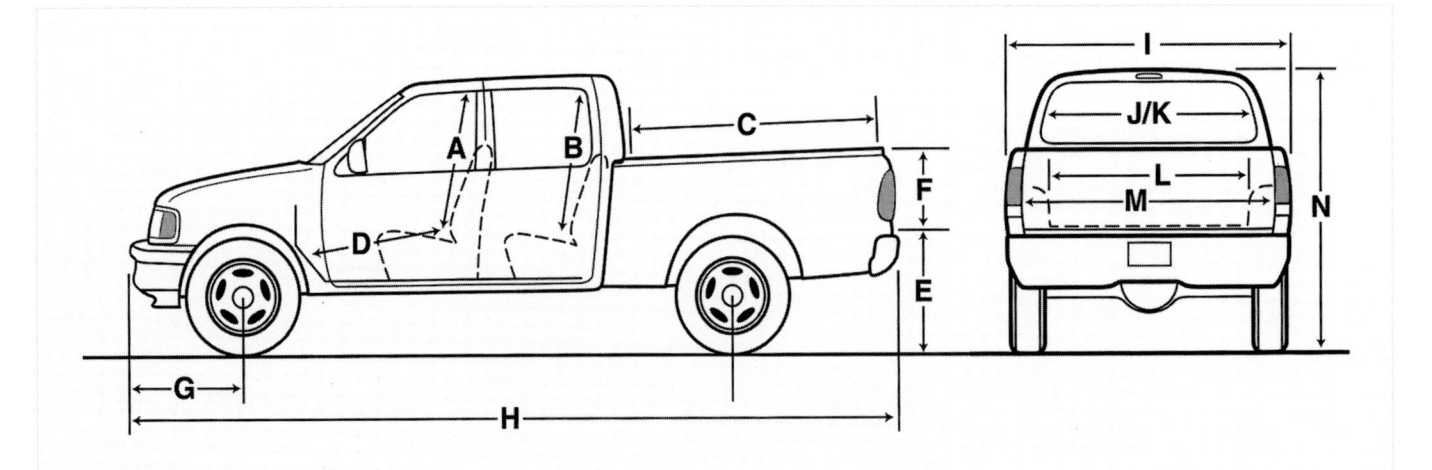

SuperCrew

Model		SuperCrew	
Drive		4x2	4x4
Wheelbase (in.)		138.5	138.8
Code	Description	Inches	Inches
A	Head Room (Front)	39.8	39.8
B	Head Room (Rear)	39.8	39.8
C	Inside Box Length[1]	67.2	67.2
D	Leg Room (Front)	41.0	41.0
	Leg Room (Rear)	36.8	36.8
E	Load Height (Empty)[2]	32.0	35.0
	Load Height (Loaded)[2]	27.4	30.5
F	Inside Height[1]	20.2	20.2
G	Front Overhang	38.7	38.7
H	Overall Length	225.9	226.2
I	Width (Max.)	79.1	79.9
J	Shoulder Room (Front)	63.7	63.7
	Shoulder Room (Rear)	63.6	63.6
K	Hip Room (Front)	59.8	59.8
	Hip Room (Rear)	58.0	58.0
L	Width Between Wheelhouses[1]	50.0	50.0
M	Max. Load Width[1]	57.7	57.7
N	Cab Height (Empty)[2]	73.9	76.9

(1) Pickup box. Also refer to Pickup Box Dimensions.
(2) The height data shown represents dimensions of a nominal vehicle with no options. Actual height may vary due to production tolerances.

Fuel Tank Capacity

Wheelbase (in.)	Availability	Location	Capacity (gallons)
138.5, 138.8	Standard Tank	Midship	25.0

Cargo Volume

Pickup Box (ft.)	Volume (cu. ft.)
5.5	44.2

NOTE: Does not include allowances for wheelhouses.

Specifics of the body dimensions of the 2001 F-150 SuperCrew. (Author's collection)

Dimensions of the 2001 F-150 SuperCrew's pickup box. Use of the bed extender added nearly 18 inches to the cargo body's overall length. (Author's collection)

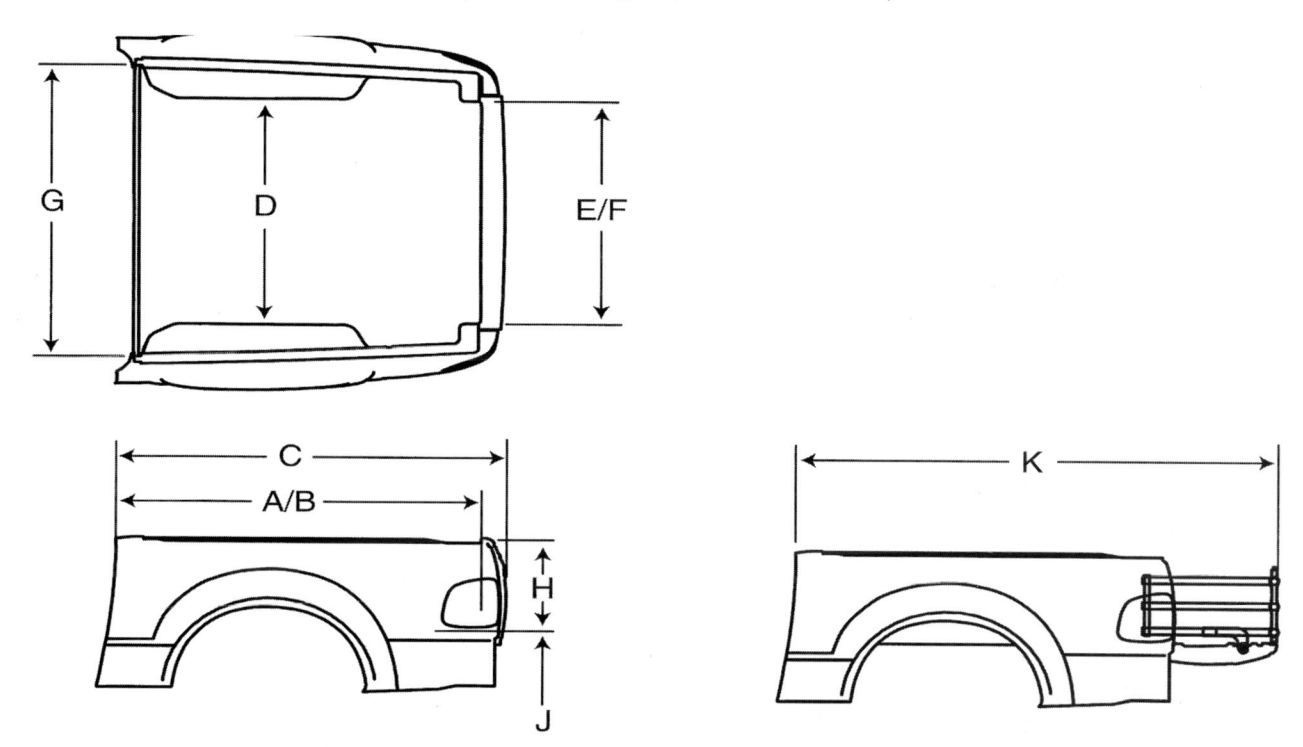

SuperCrew Pickup

Box Size (ft.)		5.5[1]
Rear Wheels		SRW
Code	Description	Inches
A	Cargo Body Length @ Floor	67.2
B	Cargo Body Length @ Top	65.5
C	Cargo Body Overall Length	70.2
D	Cargo Width @ Wheelhouse	50.0
E	Rear Opening Width @ Floor	49.3
F	Rear Opening Width @ Belt	49.3
G	Cargo Body Maximum Inside Width	57.7
H	Cargo Body Height With Molding	20.2
J	Wheelhouse Height	9.6
K	Cargo Body Overall Length w/Bed Extender Deployed	87.9

(1) On 138.5", 138.8" wheelbase SuperCrew.

Base Curb Weights

Model	WB (in.)	Cab Style	GVWR (lbs.)	Front (lbs.)	Rear (lbs.)	Total (lbs.)
4x2	138.5	SuperCrew	6350	2640	1941	4581
			6600	2710	1987	4697
4x4	138.8	SuperCrew	6500	2911	2003	4914
			6750	2981	2051	5032

Two views of the 2001 F-150 SuperCrew's standard rear 40/60 splitbench seat. As seen here, the seat backs folded flat for added cargo space. (courtesy of Ford Media Services)

overhead console was optional. This was a pickup truck first in the under-8500lb GVW segment. An optional audio-video entertainment system with VCR was available for the rear compartment.

Initially, the SuperCrew was available with the same exterior colors offered for the 2000 F-150. The Metallic Clearcoat selection consisted of Harvest Gold, Chestnut Toreador Red, Deep Wedgewood Blue, Island Blue, Amazon Green, and Silver. Clearcoat colors were Bright Red and Oxford White. A lower body two-tone paint scheme was optional. Three interior colors were offered: Medium Graphite, Medium Parchment, and Dark Graphite.

The SuperCrew was built in Ford's Kansas City Assembly Plant in Missouri. Ford Dealerships began selling the SuperCrew in February, 2000. Prices (including destination and delivery charges) of the SuperCrew began at $26,755 for the 4x2 XLT to 31,790 for the Lariat 4x4.

All 2001 models shared a number of interior improvements as well as revisions of their standard equipment content. Seat integrated restraints and a manual passenger lumbar were added to SuperCabs with 60/40 split bench seats and Captain's Chairs. Child seat tethers were provided on all regular car pickups with Captain's Chairs.

Replacing Amazon Green and Harvest Gold as available Clearcoat Metallic exterior colors were Dark Highland Green and Arizona Beige.

Interior trim revisions began with the addition of Dark Graphite for XL vinyl and cloth bench seats. The XL bench seat was not available with Medium Graphite. No longer offered

The 5.4 liter SOHC16-valve V-8 was optional for the 2001 F-150 SuperCrew. (Courtesy of Ford Media Services)

was Dark Denim Blue. If desired, Lariats could be ordered with the carpet delete option.

With its inclusion into the standard equipment of the base XL models, 4WABS became standard across the F-series line. Child seat tethers were also installed on all models.

The standard audio systems of the XL and XLT trucks were upgraded. A cassette player with clock and four speakers was added to the XL's AM/FM stereo radio, and a single CD AM/FM stereo radio with premium sound and four speakers replaced the XLT's cassette radio. A new Rear Seat Entertainment System was available for XLT and Lariat SuperCrews. New 17in cast aluminum ten-spoke wheel was added to the XLT Sport Group Option.

Power adjustable accelerator and brake pedals that were standard for the SuperCrew were also standard on all Lariats and optional for the XL and XLT.

Replacing the Work Series trucks was a new Work Truck Option for XL models which changed the XL's content in this manner:

Argent replaced chrome on the front and rear bumpers.

Storm Gray replaced chrome for the grille surround.

Argent replaced chrome on the wheel hubs.

56

This promotional piece was provided to Ford dealers to help them sell the 2001 F-150 SuperCrew. (Author's collection)

A promotional view of the 2001 F-150 SuperCrew with its bed extender in use. This was a "late availability" option for the SuperCrew and provided the user with a 7ft bed. (Author's collection)

The standard XL cloth bench sear was replaced by a vinyl unit.

F-150s with this option were badged as XL models and had the same door trim panels as the XL. Added to the 4x4 Work Option Group were All-Terrain tires. Ford advised its dealers that "We believe your work truck customers will appreciate getting more added content in their trucks-including under hood light, dual map lights, map pockets indoor trim panels, and a nicer XL wheel".

Ford's largesse had limits; this option could not be ordered for Flareside models. Nor could Work Trucks be equipped with aluminum wheels, the 40/60 split bench seat, carpeting, fog lights, the Convenience Group, single or 6-CD changer, tu-tone paint, and the Sport Truck option.

For keen F-150 enthusiasts, who delighted in mastering the subtle aspects of annual changes, the latest model offered many challenges. The wheel lips on the XL trucks were now Storm Gray instead of black. An overhead console was no longer found on XLs equipped with the Convenience Group. The XL carpeting option now included color-keyed floor mats (front and rear SuperCab). Now optional for the XLT and Lariat were heated driver and outboard passenger seats. Many changes were made in the XLT model. Carpeted, color-keyed, and monogrammed floor mats were made standard. Front and rear mats were provided for SuperCab and SuperCrew XLTs, as was a remote entry system with two key fobs and a color-keyed leather-wrapped tilt steering wheel.

The full-size doors of the 2001 F-150 SuperCrew provided what Ford claimed was "the most convenient entry and exit of any pickup in its class". (Courtesy of Ford Media Services)

The 2001 F-150 SuperCrew. "Customers said," reported Ford, "they'd be willing to accept a shorter pickup box for more room in the cab to seat six adults comfortably." (Courtesy of Ford Media Services)

The rear door of the 2001 F-150 SuperCrew contained a cup holder and map pocket. (Courtesy of Ford Media Services)

Added to the Lariat's content were dual lighted visor vanity mirrors and a electrochromic mirror. Optional for both the Lariat and XLT were new heated driver and outboard passenger seats. A 6-disc CD changer was available on SuperCabs with the 60/40 Split Bench Seat. A Moonroof was also offered for the SuperCab.

Seat Integrated Restraints (SIR) were added to both the 60/40 Split Bench Seat and the Captain's Chairs. All 60/40 split bench seats and captain chairs had a standard manual lumbar control.

The standard engine for the Regular Cab and SuperCab models continued to be the 4.2 liter ohv V-6 with 202hp and 252lb/ft of torque.

When the first Harley-Davidson F-150 had been introduced, Ford had announced that succeeding versions would be based on a different F-150 model. Making good on this promise, both the Harley-Davidson Special Edition, as well as the new King Ranch Edition F-150, were available only in SuperCrew form. This provided avid F-150/Harley-Davidson enthusiasts

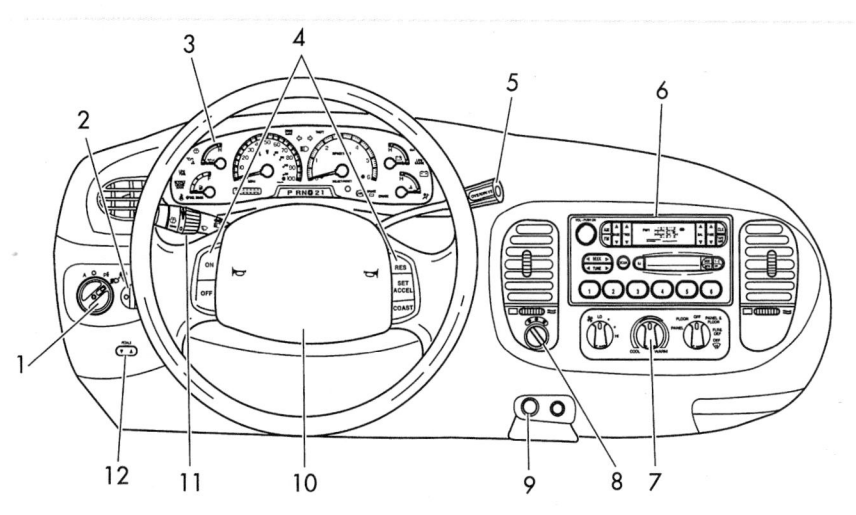

1. Headlamp control
2. Instrument panel dimmer switch
3. Instrument cluster
4. Speed control
5. Automatic transmission gearshift lever with overdrive lockout switch
6. Audio system controls
7. Climate controls
8. 4WD control(1)
9. Auxiliary front power point
10. Driver airbag
11. Turn signal, washer control and high-beam switch
12. Power adjustable brake and accelerator switch

(1) If equipped.

Details and identification of the 2001 F-150 SuperCrew instrument panel. (Author's collection)

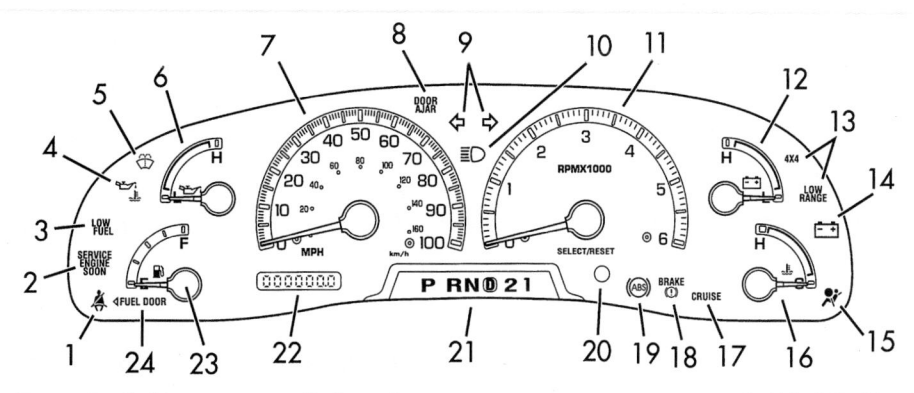

1. Fasten safety belt warning light
2. Service engine soon warning light
3. Low fuel warning light
4. Oil pressure/engine coolant temperature warning light
5. Low windshield washer fluid light
6. Engine oil pressure gauge
7. Speedometer
8. Door ajar warning light
9. Turn signal indicators
10. High-beam indicator light
11. Tachometer
12. Voltmeter
13. 4x4 system indicator lights(1)
14. Charging system warning light
15. Airbag readiness indicator/ warning light
16. Engine coolant temperature gauge
17. Speed control indicator light
18. Brake system warning light/ parking brake
19. Anti-lock Braking System warning light
20. Trip odometer/select/reset button
21. Automatic transmission gearshift indicator
22. Odometer/trip odometer
23. Fuel gauge
24. Fuel door location reminder

(1) If equipped.

A closer look at the standard tachometer of the 2001 F-150 SuperCrew instrument panel. (Author's collection)

59

The 2001 F-150 SuperCrew combined a 5½-foot pickup box with a cab that was approximately 12 inches longer than a SuperCab. Both the molded running boards and power sliding rear window were included in the $995 Lariat Upgrade Accessories Group option. (Courtesy of Ford Media Services)

The interior of a 2001 F-150 Lariat SuperCrew with the optional Captain's Chairs and console. (Courtesy of Ford Media Services)

the opportunity to own a complete set of highly collectible trucks. This would not be an easy task since Ford planned to produce no more than 12,000 Harley-Davidson F-150s for 2001.

Intent on sustaining the interest generated by the first model, Ford asserted that "other than their motorcycle, this limited-edition SuperCrew is the only vehicle the true Harley-Davidson aficionado would want to drive! Its bold black-and-chrome Harley-Davidson identification and 'In Your Face' performance perfectly complement the 'Authentic American Muscle' image these motorcycles have built over the years."

As it had with the original Harley-Davidson F-150 model, Ford selected the Sturgis, South Dakota Motorcycle Rally to introduce its successor. Speaking at the rally, Jack Turner, Ford of Canada brand manager for SuperCrew, depicted the new model as "a bold truck with attitude. The Harley-Davidson F-150 SuperCrew delivers the best of two worlds. With its four full-size doors it offers comfort, utility, and style in a truck that looks great and is Built Ford Tough."

Obviously pleased with the latest model's appearance, Harley-Davidson's chairman and CEO, Jeff Bleustein, declared that "this beautiful truck is everything an enthusiast could want, reflecting the experience and individuality of both Harley-Davidson and Ford customers".

The Harley-Davidson F-150, which was built at Ford's Kansas City assembly plant was offered only as a 4x2 Lariat, priced at $34,495 price ($33,780 MSRP plus $715 destination and delivery charges). It retained the previous model's standard features along with unique quad Captain's Chairs with black leather trim and Harley-Davidson badges. Its options were priced as follows:

Moonroof	$810
6-disc CD changer	$295
Heated front seats	$245
Sliding rear window	$125
Engine block heater	$125
Pickup bed extender	$250

As was done with the Harley-Davidson F-150, Ford linked its new King Ranch F-150 with an icon of America culture, in this case the wide open spaces of the West. "Founded in 1853", Ford said, "the legendary King Ranch sprawls across more than 800,000 acres in South Texas - larger than the entire state of Rhode Island. It is to America's ranching industry what Ford is to pickups - a respected leader ... with a long-standing, hard-earned reputation for quality and integrity. The perfect name to link with a versatile, hard-working F-150 SuperCrew equipped to a new level of luxury."

The descendants of the ranch's founder, Richard King, still owned and operated the ranch, which began in an area ranking among America's most remote, most harsh and most beautiful regions. The Ranch's accomplishments included developing the first American breed of cattle (Santa Gretrudis), being a source of high quality running horses, and a leading breeder of quarter and cut horses. Its success in raising cattle in severe conditions contributed to improved livestock production techniques and wildlife management.

In announcing the latest F-150, Gene Brown, Ford Division's F-150 marketing manager, explained, "F-150 and King Ranch are both very strong trailblazers in their fields, and it made sense for us to partner with them to build this truck as a reminder of the history that we share in getting the job done, no matter what challenges we face.

"We looked at a number of brands in deciding upon a relationship that would make sense for both parties. We are very proud of the F-150 SuperCrew and feel that King Ranch is the right association for our most upscale product offering."

The logic of Ford's association with the King Ranch was undergirded by Ford's dominance of the truck market in the Southwest. As early as

Left, from top to bottom: The optional Captain's Chairs and console for the XLT SuperCrew; The standard front 40/60 split bench seat for the XLT SuperCrew. A manual lumbar support was included for both driver and passenger. All SuperCrews had a fold-down rear split bench seat. The XLT seats were cloth-finished and were offered in Medium Graphite, Medium Parchment or Dark Graphite; The standard front 60/40 split bench seat for the Lariat SuperCrew; The optional Captain's Chairs with console for the Lariat SuperCrew. All Lariats had leather seating surfaces, front and rear. The driver's seat was powered and both front seats had lumber supports. The driver seat's unit was powered. Lariat seats were offered in either Medium Graphite or Medium Parchment. (Author's collection)

1998 this was the number one retail truck sales region in the US. During that year Ford's Southwest Region dealers sold over 115,610 F-series pickups. This was the first time any manufacturer had sold over 100,000 retail units.

For his part, King Ranch President, Jack Hunt, had only words of praise and enthusiasm for this venture: "King Ranch is excited about the partnership with Ford on the F-150 SuperCrew. Like Ford trucks, King Ranch is known for quality, toughness and innovation".

King Ranch standard equipment included a 4.6 liter V-8, electronic 4-speed automatic overdrive transmission, 4-wheel disc brakes with 4-wheel ABS, remote keyless entry with driver's side key pad, power adjustable pedals, electronic shift-on-the-fly (4x4 only), power driver's seat, heated front seats, (cushion and seat back), 6-disc CD changer with AM/FM premium cassette and clock (included speed-compensated volume control), color-keyed two-tone leather-wrapped steering wheel, electrochromic mirror, lighted vanity mirror, HomeLink with TravelNote, sliding rear window, P275/60R17 All-Season OWL tires (4x2), P265/70R17 All-Terrain OWL tires (4x4), fog lamps, power mirrors with integrated turn signals (body color skull caps), wheel-lip moldings (accent color), chrome front bumper with accent color top and valance, body-color grille surround, and mesh grille (accent color).

Many unique and unusual features were exclusive to the King Ranch. A dark brown saddle-grade Castano leather, which was twice as thick as the leather usually used for vehicle interiors, trimmed its front and rear Captain's Chairs. Just in case a customer for the King Ranch F-150 was curious about the characteristics of Castano leather, Ford suggested that sales representatives "Share this info with customers who want to know more: tanning the hides with natural oils and dyes and then retanning gives the leather a pebbled texture and a natural variation.

"You can even see tick marks and scratches in the hide.

"The rich aroma of this leather is one of its most striking features.

"Expect the reddish-brown color to change over time, just as any fine leather, lightening in the sun and darkening with wear.

"Just like saddles, boots and gloves on the ranch, this leather will become more supple to fit the users as time passes."

The seats were also embossed with the King Ranch logo (based on the ranch's famous branding iron design) and fitted with 2-way head restraints. Additional interior appointments included front and rear consoles with leather-covered armrests/lids and front and rear floor mats with embroidered King Ranch logo. The seat back pockets had flaps suggestive of those used on vintage saddlebags.

Ten-spoke 17 x 7.5in painted aluminum wheels and lighted running boards (accent color), both unique to the King Ranch, highlighted its exterior. Additional distinctive features were a two-tone paint with raised curline and tape break stripes, King Ranch F-150 fender badges, and accent color box rail moldings

Available King Ranch options

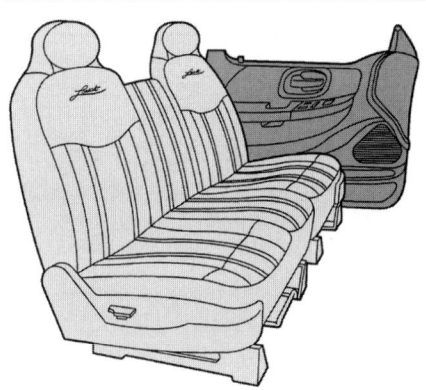

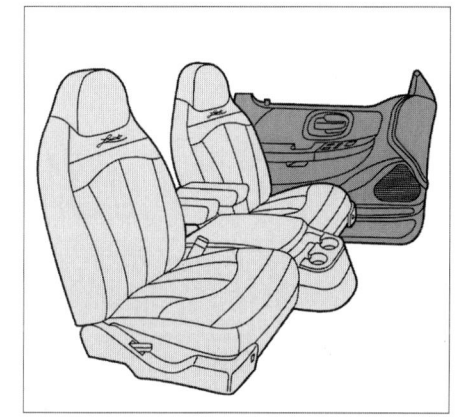

This 16 x 7in, 5-lug polished aluminum wheel with a chrome hub cover was standard for the 2001 XLT F-150 SuperCrew. A 16in steel spare wheel was provided. (Author's collection)

Optional for the 2001 XLT SuperCrew F-150 was this 16 x 7in 5-lug, 5-spoke cast aluminum wheel with a chrome hub cover. A 16in steel spare wheel was provided. (Author's collection)

Optional for the 4x4 2001 XLT SuperCrew was this 17 x 7.5in 5-lug, 10-spoke cast aluminum wheel with a chrome hub cover. A 17in steel spare was included. Optional P265/70r10 OWL All-Terrain tires were required. (Author's collection)

The standard 17 x 7.5in, 5-lug chrome steel wheel with a chrome hub cover for the 2001 Lariat F-150 SuperCrew. A 17in steel spare wheel was provided. (Author's collection)

consisted of a power moon roof (not available with rear seat entertainment center), pickup bed extender, skid plates (4x4 only), 4x4 Off-Road Group, Trailer Tow Package, $1295 Rear Seat Entertainment Package (not available with power moon roof), limited slip axle, and 5.4 liter SEFI V-8 (260hp/350ft.lb of torque). Additional extra-cost equipment included a King Ranch bed liner, King Ranch tonneau cover and King Ranch splash guards.

Three clearcoat metallic exterior colors, all in combination with an Arizona Beige tu-tone arrangement, were unique to the King Ranch: Chestnut, Charcoal Blue, and Estate Green. The initial MSRP prices of the two King Ranch models, including destination and delivery were $30,910 (4x2) and $34,365 (4x4).

Ford introduced the 2001 Lightning on October 31, 2000 at the 35th Annual SEMA show in Las Vegas. Neither John Coletti, nor Tom Scarpello, were shy when it came to touting the latest Lightning's virtues. "The 2001 SVT Lightning gives owners everything they have learned to love, but more of it", said Coletti. "It's the most powerful, best-handling one we've yet produced and some dramatic design changes make this 2001 model instantly recognizable."

Keeping the tempo going, Scarpelo added, "This is a performance truck that hits its market niche target right in the bull's-eye. We design and engineer these vehicles for discriminating enthusiasts who know what they want and expect. Our plan is to keep meeting or exceeding their expectations, and this vehicle will just keep getting better and better. That's the way it has to be, particularly for this customer."

It came as no surprise, then, that the 2001 version of the F-150 Lightning had a more powerful engine, with 380hp@4750rpm and 450lb/ft of torque @3250rpm. These increases were achieved by use of a front air intake opening that was 50 per cent larger than in 2000, a larger, by 26 per cent, air inlet opening in the filter box, improvements in the intercooler's efficiency, and a redesigned lower intake manifold. In addition, more cooling tubes were added to the intercooler below the supercharger.

Handling was upgraded by the use of monotube Bilstein gas-charged shock absorbers. Other changes included the use of a stronger 4.5in aluminum drive shaft in place of the 3.5in steel unit used on the previous model. A 3.73:1 axle ratio replaced the 3.55:1 ratio of 2000. The use of a new rubber compound improved the adhesion of the Lightning's 295/45ZR-18 Goodyear Eagle F1-GS tires.

Numerous exterior changes, additions, and upgrades set the appearance of the 2001 Lightning apart from the 2000 model's.

Both the upper and lower grille segments had new horizontal bars. The headlights, tail-lights, side-marker lights and fog lights all had clear, crystalline lenses. The cab's center, high-mounted stop lamp had ten light-emitting diodes flanked by two clear-lens cargo lights. The Lightning's 18x9.5in cast aluminum wheels were given a "sharper-edged design" for 2001.

The most significant interior change involved the sun visors, which now included lighted vanity mirrors and side blades extendible to the side windows for additional shade protection.

Ford's official performance data for the 2001 Lightning was impressive:

0-60mph	5.8sec
0-100km/hr	5.9sec
Standing-start ¼ mile	
0-100mph	13.9sec
0-100-0mph	22.0sec
Top speed	142mph*

Maximum speeds in the gears:

cont'd p64

This model identification was located on the lower left hand side of the 2001 F-150 SuperCrew's tailgate. (Courtesy of Ford Media Services)

The 2001 F-150 SuperCrew's standard 17in chromed steel wheels are shown to good advantage in this view. (Courtesy of Ford Media Services)

A bird's eye comparison of the 2001 F-150 SuperCrew and SuperCab. The SuperCrew's power moon roof was an $810 option. (Courtesy of Ford Media Services)

A 2001 F-150 SuperCab Lariat. The Lariat model was not available as a Regular Cab F-150 for 2001. The chromed steel wheels and 17in OWL tires were new for 2001. The black side steps on this F-150 were optional. (Courtesy of Ford Media Services)

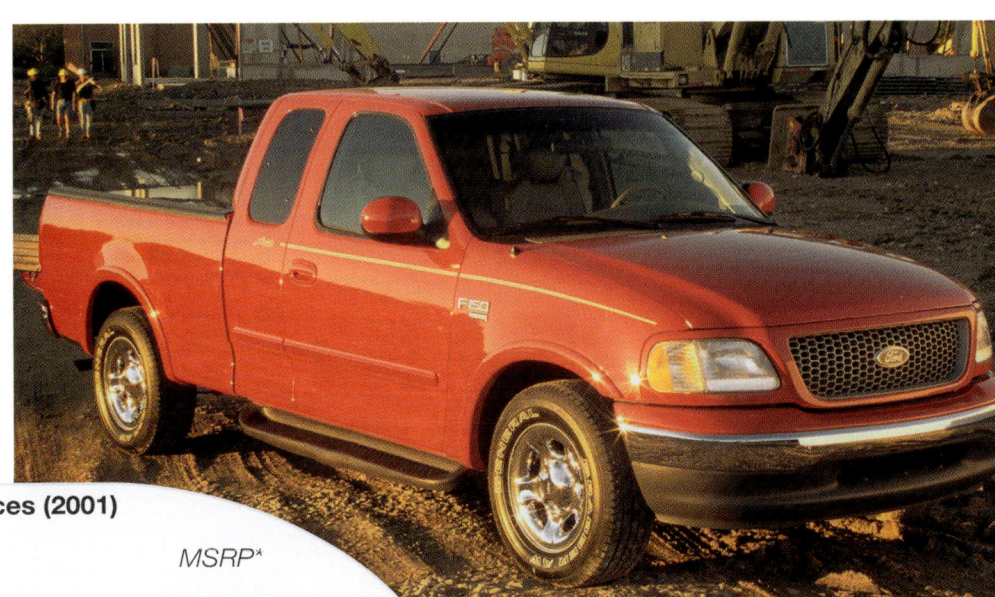

F-150 model and option prices (2001)

Model	MSRP*
Styleside Regular Cab	
4x2 XL, 120in wb	$17,245
4x2 XLT, 120in wb	$20,225
4x2 XL, 139in wb	$17,545
4x2 XLT, 139in wb	$20,520
4x4 XL, 120in wb	$20,585
4x4 XLT, 120in wb	$23,640
4x4, XL, 139in wb	$20,885
4x4, XLT, 139in wb	$23,950
Flareside Regular Cab	
4x2 XL, 120in wb	$18,255
4x2 XLT, 120in wb	$21,235
4x4 XL, 120in wb	$21,595
4x4 XLT, 120in wb	$24,650
Styleside SuperCab	
4x2, XL, 139in wb	$19,895
4x2, XLT, 139in wb	$23,070
4x2, Lariat, 139in wb	$26,590
4x2, XL, 157in wb	$20,195
4x2, XLT, 157in wb	$23,370
4x2 Lariat, 157in wb	$26,890
4x4 XL, 139in wb	$23,760
4x4 XLT, 139in wb	$26,880
4x4 Lariat, 139in wb	$29,885
4x4 XL, 157in wb	$24,060
4x4 XLT, 157in wb	$27,180
4x4 Lariat, 157in wb	$30,185
Flareside SuperCab	
4x2 XL, 139in wb	$20,905
4x2 XLT, 139in wb	$24,080
4x2 Lariat, 139in wb	$27,600
4x4 XL, 139in wb	$24,770
4x4 XLT, 139in wb	$27,895
4x4 Lariat, 139in wb	$30,895
Styleside SuperCrew	
4x2 XLT, 139in wb	$26,915
4x2 Lariat, 139in wb	$28,450
4x2 King Ranch, 139in wb	$30,950
4x2 Harley Davidson Edition, 139in wb	$33,780

continued next page

First	43mph
Second	76mph
Third	119mph
Fourth	142mph
Braking	
60mph-0mph	136ft
80mph-0mph	238ft
Speed through an 80ft slalom	
	63.8mph
100ft skid pad	0.85g

*The engine's redline was 5250rpm. Fuel shut off at 5400rpm limited the top speed to this level.

Ford's production schedule for the 2001 Lightning called for 7500 units, up from the 5000 level of 2000. The Lightning's MSRP, including a $715 destination and delivery charge, was $32,300. The only option was a soft tonneau cover for the bed, priced at $150.

Ford's durability testing of the 2001 F-150 included a sequence simulating 100,000 'real life' miles of operation. It has these elements:

Chuckhole testing on a 240-foot road with potholes of various depths.

An 800-foot stretch of sand eight inches deep.

A 'bath' of salt and mud to test corrosion protection.

	MSRP*
4x4 XLT,139in wb	$30,130
4x4 Lariat,139in wb	$31,905
4x4 King Ranch, 130-in wb	$34,405
*Destination and delivery was an additional	$715

Options and equipment	Price
Engines	
4.6 liter V-8	$750
5.4 liter V-8	
4x4 SuperCab, All SuperCrew and Lariat	$800
All other	$1550
Transmission	
Electronic Automatic Overdrive	$1095
Axles	
Optional axle ratio upgrade	$50
Limited slip rear axle	$285
Tires	
Regular/SuperCab 4x2	
P235/70R x 16 OWL All-Season (XL/XLT)	$125
P255/70R x 16 OWL All-Season (XL/XLT)	$295
Regular/SuperCab 4x4	
P235/70R x 16 OWL All-Season (XL/XLT)	$125
P255/70R x 16 OWL All-Terrain (XL/XLT)	$400
P255/70R x 16 OWL All-Terrain (with XL Spt. Grp.)	$125
LT245/75R x 16 OWL All-Terrain(with XL/XLT)	$695
LT265/70R x 17 OWL All-Terrain	$300
SuperCrew XLT 4x2	
P255/70R x 16 OWL All-Season	$125
SuperCrew XLT 4x4	
P255/70R16SL OWL All-Terrain	$125
P265/70R17 OL All-Terrain	$340
LT245/75R16D All-Terrain	$400
Seats	
XL	
Vinyl Bench	NC
40/60 Split Bench	$400
XLT	
Captain's Chairs with Console	$490
Lariat	
Captain's Chairs with Console	$490
Heated Seats	$245
*Additional Options**	
Payload Package #2 (Work Series)	$470
Payload Package #3 (Work Series)	$470
Payload Package #2 (XL/XLT)	$270
Payload Package #3 (XL/XLT)	$270
7700 Payload Package	$1295
4x4 Off-Road Equipment Group (Lariat)	$450
4x4 Off-Road Equipment Group (XLT)	$995
Rear Seat VHS Equipment	$1295
Air Conditioning	$805
Pickup Bed Extender (SuperCrew)	$195
Black Platform Cab Steps	
(4x2 Styleside, all SuperCrew):	$250
Black Tubular Cab Steps (4x2 Styleside, all Flareside)	$350
Convenience Group Credit (XL on;only)	(-$55)
Diamond Plate Accessories Package	$995

continued over

Near the end of the 2001 model year run, several improvements were adopted that were carried over into 2002. New seat bolsters were used on SuperCab and SuperCrew 60/40 split bench seats and Captain's Chairs. Ford explained that they provided "added comfort and support". Availability of the Lariat upgrade package was extended to the SuperCrew. Seat Integrated Restraints (SIR) were added to the SuperCab 60/40 bench seat and Captain's Chairs. A manual passenger lumbar was added to all 60/40 bench seat and Captain's Chairs. Child seat tethers became standard as follows: (one in front seat with Captain's Chairs, two in front seat with bench seat, and three in rear seat of SuperCabs with exception of 60/40 bench seat option which has only one tether). Rear head restraints were added to SuperCrews.

It might have been the day after Christmas, but on December 26, 2001, Ford was more interested in celebrations of another sort. "When it comes to silver anniversaries", said a Ford spokesperson, "people often think about weddings. But for Ford, a silver anniversary inspires thoughts of something else: trucks". Specifically, the F-150 celebrated two anniversaries at year's end: its 25th as the best-selling truck in the US and its 20th as America's best-selling vehicle, car or truck.

"This is an unprecedented milestone in the automotive industry - maybe any industry", said Jim O'Connor, Ford Division President. "F-series is the foundation of the Ford franchise. Celebrating the silver anniversary of truck sales leadership is a testament to

Option	Price
Electric Shift-On-the Fly, 4x4 (XLT/Lariat)	$160
Fog Lamps	$140
Front Tow Hooks (4x4 XL)	$40
Heavy-Duty Electrical/Cooling Group	$210
Lariat Upgrade Package	$995
Power Moonroof (SuperCab and SuperCrew)	$810
Lower Accent Two-Tone Paint	$225
Power Adjustable Driver's Pedals (XL/XLT)	$120
Power Driver's Seat/Autolamp (XLT)	$360
Skid Plates (Regular Cab SWB, 4x4)	$80
Skid Plates (All other 4x4)	$160
Speed Control/Tilt Steering Wheel	$385
Sport Group (XL 4x2)	$495
Sport Group (XL 4x4)	$595
Sport Group (XLT 4x2)	$595
Sport Group (XLT 4x4)	$595
Top 3 Accessories Package	$750
Trailer Towing Group, Class III	$350
Polished Aluminum Wheels (XL)	$200
Cast Aluminum Wheels (XLT)	NC
Sliding Rear Window	$125
Soft Tonneau Cover	$150
Work Truck Group	(-$400)
Electronic AM/FM Stereo/Clock/Cassette (Reg. Cab/SuperCab/XLT)	(-$90)
Electronic AM/FM Stereo/Clock/Single CD Player (XL)	$190
CD Changer, 6-Disc with AM/FM Premium Stereo Cassette (XLT/Lariat)	$295
Limited Production Options	
5.4 liter Natural Gas Engine	$7225
5.4 liter EFI Bi-Fuel Prep. Engine	$1565
Bi-Fuel Prep. Natural Gas (CNG)	$5995
Bi-Fuel Prep. Propane (LPG)	$5995
Fuel Tank, In-Bed Dual with Natural Gas option	$135
Carpet Delete (with XLT or Lariat trim)	($50)
Daytime Running Lights (Fleet only)	$45
Engine Block Heater	$90

*Available on all models unless otherwise noted

our Built Ford Tough truck heritage."

A few days later, on January 3, 2002, Ford had more good news about its truck's popularity. US customers had purchased or leased 911,597 F-series trucks in 2001, establishing a new industry truck sales record. The old record, 876,716, had been set by the F-series in 2000.

Leading the list of refinements and revisions for 2002 was a new FX4 Off Road package for XLT and Lariat. Its content included 17in, five-spoke cast aluminum wheels with exposed stainless steel lug nuts, white colored Rancho branded shock absorbers, 3:55:1 axle ratio, red and white-colored Rancho shock absorbers, skid plates for fuel tank, transfer case, and frame front member, and P265/70R17 outline white letter tires (including spare). Optional LT265/70R17 OWL All-Terrain tires were recommended for demanding off-road use.

Exterior identification consisted of FX4 decals and tape stripes. A unique Dark Shadow Gray lower body color was listed for the XLT to create a two-tone color scheme. In conjunction with the Dark Shadow Gray color, six exterior colors were offered: True Blue Clearcoat Metallic, Black Clearcoat, Oxford White Clearcoat, Silver Clearcoat Metallic, Toreador Red Clearcoat Metallic, and Bright Red Clearcoat Metallic. Arizona Beige was specified to create the same effect for the Lariat.

Accordingly, depending on trim level, the wheel lip moldings, bumper, grille insert, and lower valance were Arizona Beige or Dark Shadow Gray.

All models were now equipped with a spare tire lock and a new ISO symbol loose fuel cap warning light. Air con. became standard for the XL. It was deleted from the Work Truck Group but was still available as an option.

The power adjustable accelerator and brake pedals that were standard for the 2001 SuperCrew were now made standard for all Lariat models and optional for XL and XLT trucks.

Improving the F-150's versatility was the availability of All-Terrain tires with the 4x4 Work truck option. Available for 4x2 models only was a new upgraded 7700lb Payload Package B. It included a 4.10:1 axle ratio, one-piece, 4.5in drive shaft, and a Class III Trailer Tow package. It increased the truck's GCW from 13,500lb to 15,000lb.

Estate Green Clearcoat Metallic was now offered for XLT and Lariat models. Lariats could also be ordered in Toreador Red. Two new exterior colors, True Blue Clearcoat Metallic and Dark Shadow Gray, replaced Deep Wedgewood Blue and Island Blue. The remaining Clearcoat Metallic exterior colors for 2002 were Arizona Beige, Chestnut, Toreador Red, Medium Charcoal Blue, True Blue, Dark Highland Green, Estate Green, and Silver. Available Clearcoat colors were Bright Red, Black, and Oxford White.

All F-150 engines were improved to give quieter engine operation. The

The interior of a 2001 F-150 SuperCab Lariat with the optional Captain's Chairs. (Courtesy of Ford Media Services)

During the 2001 model year, Ford offered the F-150 XLT Regular Cab with the $595 XLT Sport Group at no extra charge. Its features consisted of a Storm Grey mesh grille with color-keyed surround, color-keyed front and rear bumpers and top cap, color-keyed power mirror caps, Dark Graphite 40/60 bench seat or optional, at $490, Captain's Chairs with console with unique material and sew style, P275/60Rx 17 All-Season OWL tires (4x2) or P265/70R x 17 All-Terrain OWL tires (4x4), 17in 10-spoke cast aluminum wheels, 3.55:1 rear axle, and either a 'SPORT' decal (4x2), or '4X4 SPORT'. Four exterior colors were available: Bright Red Clearcoat, Black Clearcoat, Silver Clearcoat Metallic, and Oxford White Clearcoat. (Author's collection)

The 2001 F-150 SuperCab's four doors provided pillarless access to the rear seating area. (Courtesy of Ford Media Services)

This F-150 identification is from the tailgate of a 2001 F-150 Lariat SuperCab. (Courtesy of Ford Media Services)

A 2001 F-150 Lariat SuperCab in Bright Red. The 17in chromed steel wheels were exclusive to the Lariat. (Courtesy of Ford Media Services)

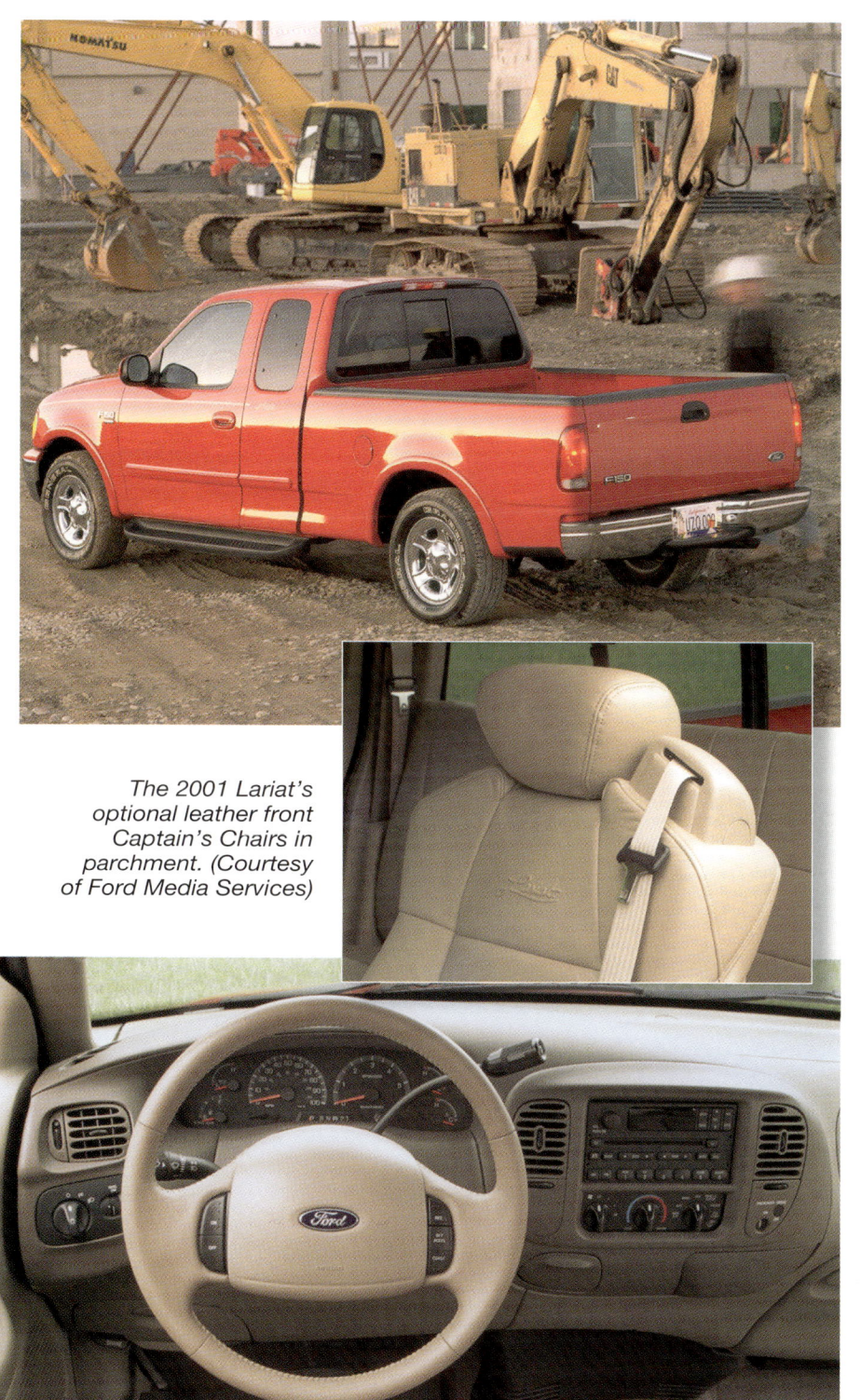

The 2001 F-150 Lariat SuperCab. The molded running boards and power sliding rear window on this F-150 were included in the $995 Lariat Upgrade Accessories Group option. (Courtesy of Ford Media Services)

The 2001 Lariat's optional leather front Captain's Chairs in parchment. (Courtesy of Ford Media Services)

The 2001 F-150 Lariat steering wheel and dash assembly. The steering wheel mounted, illuminated fingertip electronic speed control was standard, both for the Lariat and XLT. (Courtesy of Ford Media Services)

4.2 liter engine was now Ultra Low Emissions Vehicle (ULEV) compliant. The 5.4 liter bi-fuel engine was now SULEV compatible. A new 6K FEAD and vistronic fan clutch were used for improved fuel economy. An engine block heater was standard for trucks destined for the state of South Dakota, North Dakota, Wisconsin, Wyoming, Arkansas, Minnesota, and Montana. It remained a dealer installed option elsewhere.

The King Ranch F-150 was now available as a SuperCrew and a SuperCab. Both had standard lighted visor mirrors with Homelink and TravelNote. The SuperCrew retained its quad Captain's Chairs, while the SuperCab was fitted with front Captain's Chairs and a rear bench seat. The SuperCrew continued to have front and rear consoles; the SuperCab had only one, at the front. SuperCrew versions were available with an optional 60/40 rear seat.

Added to the standard equipment of the King Ranch SuperCrew was electronic automatic temperature control (EATC). This feature was also now standard for the F-150 SuperCrew Lariat. During the year it also became available for the SuperCab.

Early in the model year, examples of the third version of the Harley-Davidson F-150, now in SuperCrew form, began arriving in Ford showrooms. Many of the styling cues of previous models were apparent, again emphasized by a one inch height reduction; but they were also joined by many new features, the most notable of which was found under the Ford's hood. In place of the 5.4 liter, 260hp Triton V-8 used in 2000 and 2001 was a mildly detuned version of

69

This scripted identification was placed on the 2001 Lariat's pickup box just behind the cab. (Courtesy of Ford Media Services)

the Lightning's supercharged V-8. As used in the Harley-Davidson F-150 this engine developed 340hp@4500rpm and 425lb/ft of torque @3250rpm. The same supercharger was used for both engines, but the Harley-Davidson's had a larger pulley that, by slowing the rotation speed, lowered its boost. Also setting the two engines apart were their exhaust systems. In the case of the Harley-Davidson it used a specially-tuned arrangement with a dual inlet/dual outlet muffler exiting through chrome 3½in 'slash-cut' exhaust tips to once again produce the appropriate Harley-Davidson exhaust tones.

The engine was coupled to a 4R100-HD 4-speed automatic transmission and a limited slip differential with a 3.73:1 axle ratio. Used on the latest Harley-Davidson was a two-piece drive shaft that, said Ford, reduced noise, vibration, and harshness.

Contemporary road tests indicated the H-D F-150 was, with a time of just over six seconds, about one second slower from zero to 60mph than the Ford Lightning.

Joining the Black exterior of previous models was a new Dark Shadow Gray (charcoal-gray) color. Replacing the earlier model's orange body stripe were new flame pinstripe decals that fanned out into a trail of flames as they extended onto the sides of the bed. The latest version of the front fender and tailgate badges incorporated the word 'Supercharged', written in script form.

The truck's front end appearance was freshened by use of a new body-color fascia and a chromed bar grille billet. New clear-lens head and parking lamps were embossed with the Harley-Davidson bar and shield. The 20in wheels retained this identification on their center caps which were now surrounded by a new rivet design.

The H-D F-150's cabin was updated in several areas. A restyled 'spun metal' instrument panel carried a 'Supercharged' inscription. The design of the exterior badges was embossed on the front and rear center consoles. Other interior features included brushed stainless steel and rubber pedals. Ford limited production of the 2002 Harley-Davidson to no more than 12,000 units and each truck had an individually sequenced plate attached to the front center console indicating its place in the production run. For example, the plate of the 10901 unit built read '10901/12000'.

Top executives of both Harley-Davidson and Ford had words of praise for the latest H-D-150. Ford Division president, Jim O'Connor, said "the 2002 Harley-Davidson F-150 SuperCrew has a distinct style and attitude that's all its own.

The 2001 Harley-Davidson F-150 SuperCrew. Ford told its dealers that "other than their motorcycle, the limited-edition SuperCrew is the only vehicle the true Harley-Davidson aficionado would want to drive! Its bold black-and-chrome theme, dominant 'Harley-Davidson' identification and 'In Your Face' performance perfectly complement the 'Authentic American Muscle these motorcycles have built over the years." (Courtesy of Ford Media Services)

The quad Captain's Chairs were trimmed in black leather and had jewel Harley-Davidson nameplates. (Courtesy of Ford Media Services)

Front and rear views of the 2001 Harley-Davidson F-150 SuperCrew with a Harley-Davidson motorcycle. (Courtesy of Ford Media Services)

With a supercharged engine, four full-size doors, and unique styling, this truck gives customers the image they are looking for and the comfort, convenience and power they need."

Jeff Bleustein, Harley-Davidson's CEO, added these thoughts: "This truck reflects the lifestyle and individuality of both Harley-Davidson and Ford customers. It is right at home in Sturgis, Daytona Beach, or Main street, USA."

The Harley-Davidson F-150's MSRP was $36,495. The destination charge was $715. Added to the option list for 2002 were heated front seats.

A new exterior color, True Blue Clearcoat Metallic was available for the 2002 SVT F-150 Lightning. Added to the Lightning's standard equipment was a keyless entry keypad and locking lug nuts.

For 2003, the F-150 was quieter and more refined as a result of a 75-part noise, vibration, and harshness upgrade. At 4000rpm, wide-open throttle, the F-150 interior was now more than five sones quieter. The Speech Articulation Index, a measure of how easily a conversation can take place was improved by more than ten per cent across the engine speed range.

The King Ranch F-150 (scheduled for late model year availability), was now equipped with chrome tubular running boards, a 6-disc in-dash CD changer, a woodgrain center stack bezel and door switch bezels. Oxford White and Black were added to its exterior color choices.

Standard on the Lariat and King Ranch SuperCrew models was a heated rear window. Premium Imola Leather-trimmed seats were now optional for SuperCrew models. Audio system choices were expanded to include a cassette/CD player (standard on Lariats), and the 6-disc in-dash CD changer that was standard for the King Ranch. All 2003 F-150's were equipped with the new LATCH (Lower Anchors and Tethers for Children) system. Burgundy Red Clearcoat Metallic was a new exterior color for 2003.

Two new versions of the F-150 highlighted the 2003 model year. Introduced in the latter part of 2002, the F-150 STX was, said Ford, intended for "those seeking an exclusive look". The STX package was available on XL and XLT Regular Cab and SuperCab models. Key exterior features began with 17in, five-spoke Chromtec styled wheels and new 'STX' or 'STX 4x4'

71

This 2001 Harley-Davidson F-150 was equipped with the optional pickup bed extender. The cargo box mat with its Harley-Davidson logo is clearly seen in this view. (Courtesy of Ford Media Services)

The Harley-Davidson F-150's bed extender in its stored position. (Courtesy of Ford Media Services)

The Harley-Davidson F-150 tail gate carried both the blue Ford oval and the Harley-Davidson F-150 Alliance logo. (Courtesy of Ford Media Services)

decals. Chrome tubular step bars were installed as were round fog lights and clear headlamps and parking lamps. A monochromatic exterior was offered in Burgundy Red, Silver, True Blue, Bright Red, or Oxford White. The grille was body-colored and was surrounded by a chrome ring and a black billet grille insert. The wheel-lip moldings, mirror caps, front and rear bumpers, and lower fascia were body-colored.

A 40/60 bench seat finished in Dark Graphic cloth was standard as was a premium Kenwood ZA828 audio system with CD and MP3 functionally, AM/FM stereo with clock, wireless remote control, removable faceplate, and Sirius Satellite. The center stack bezel and door plates had brushed-aluminum covers. The STX was built at Ford's Oakville, Ontario truck plant.

The second unique F-150 for 2003 was the F-150 Heritage Edition. "With the word 'heritage' in its title", it's a vehicle, said Ford, "that commemorates 100 years of truck excellence at Ford Motor Company". The Heritage F-150 was based on the SuperCab XLT Styleside model. Unique to the Heritage was a two-tone exterior with a high cut line. Veteran Ford truck watchers were aware that Ford had reached back into its past for this paint design's inspiration since it was reminiscent of those used on the 1965 F-100 and the 1974 F-100 SuperCab. The two-tone paint scheme combined a black upper section with a choice of three lower body colors: Burgundy Red, Arizona Beige and Dark Shadow Gray. A black bed liner with a Ford logo was installed as was 'HERITAGE EDITION' F-150 badging on the front fender and tailgate.

Adding distinction to the Heritage's appearance was a chrome tubular cab step, and a chrome grille surround with a black honeycomb grille insert.

The interior was highlighted by standard black split-bench seating with a lower accent color seat insert fabric option on Captain's Chairs. A front black floor mat and two-piece rear floor mats were standard.

Widely anticipated since Ford and Harley-Davidson had first joined to produce the limited edition Harley-

The 2001 King Ranch F-150 SuperCrew. Ford regarded it as "the ideal choice for successful truck customers who won't settle for anything less than the best!" (Courtesy of Ford Media Services)

The 2001 King Ranch F-150 SuperCrew "on location." The color combination is Charcoal Blue/Arizona Beige. (Courtesy of Ford Media Services)

Davidson 150 had been the 2003 version commemorating the 100th anniversary of both firms. Making note of a slight change in model nomenclature, Steve Lyons, Ford Division President, remarked that "Getting two giants of American motoring together was a natural back in 1999 when we introduced the first Ford Harley-Davidson F-150 pickup. The alliance has continued and with both Ford Motor Company and Harley-Davidson turning 100 in 2003, we thought it only fitting that we produce another special vehicle. These two companies have been around 100 years because they've produced products that meet the needs and wants of the individual customer - products that people aspire to, not only for their looks, but for quality as well. Forming alliances that strengthen the identity of each partner, such as ours with Harley-Davidson, is one of the ways we will continue to lead as we enter our second century of business".

In addition to again being available in Black, the latest version, priced at $37,295, including destination and delivery costs, was offered with an optional, high-belt-lined Black over Silver Metallic two-tone. A specially designed "Harley-Davidson 100th Anniversary F-150 Supercharged" nameplate incorporating the years 1903 and 2003 and the 100 numeral into the previous emblem was again positioned on the front fenders and tailgate. At the truck's front a new valance with fog lights was used. Also contributing to the truck's distinctive appearance were new chrome tie down hooks.

Several fresh interior features were also introduced. The centennial emblem was located on the leather-wrapped console lids. The production sequence plate read "Harley-Davidson 100th Anniversary F-150 Supercharged" and included the individually sequenced VIN plate. Both the steering wheel and door trim accents were finished in Ebony/Satin Silver. An in-dash 6-disc CD changer was included as standard equipment. The backlight was now heated.

No changes were made to the truck's supercharged engine, but the upper intake and supercharger now had a black gloss finish.

The Ford Harley-Davidson F-150 was introduced as part of the 100th Anniversary Open Road Tour, a 10-city, 13-month traveling festival ending in Milwaukee on August 31, 2003, that Harley-Davidson hosted as part of its centennial celebration. For its part, Ford donated a 2003 Harley-Davidson

A close view of the 2001 King Ranch fender badge. (Courtesy of Ford Media Services)

73

The 2001 King Ranch F-150 had front and rear leather-trimmed Captain's Chairs with embossed King Ranch logos, 2-way head restraints and front and rear consoles with leather-covered armrests/lids. (Courtesy of Ford Media Services)

All four seats of the 2001 King Ranch F-150 had these embossed King Ranch logos. (Courtesy of Ford Media Services)

F-150 to assist Harley-Davidson in reaching its goal of raising at least $5million for the Muscular Dystrophy Association.

The latest SVT F-150 Lightning received a number of technical and appearance refinements. Readily apparent were redesigned 18x9.5in five-spoke cast aluminum wheels. Dark Shadow Gray and Sonic Blue joined Oxford White, Bright Red, and Black in the Lightning's exterior color selection.

Interior changes consisted of door handles with a brushed aluminum finish, a new four-spoke steering wheel with perforated leather wrapping and thicker section-width rim, a unique air bag cover, and improved plush high-pile carpet material more resistant to wear and having improved sound insulation. A new in-dash 6-disc AM/FM/CD stereo with improved equalization provided both higher sound quality and more convenient CD changes.

What Ford represented as "tweaks to the spring rates", increased the Lightning's cargo capacity from 800 to 1400lb. A revalved steering gear had better on-center feel and reduced lash.

On August 13, 2003, the 2003 SVT Lightning was certified by Guiness World Records, Ltd. as the "World's Fastest Production Pickup Truck". Although Ford had never made this assertion, it had been a popular depiction of the Lightning by many automotive journalists. The record run took place on the five mile, high speed oval of Ford's Michigan Proving Grounds. In order for the run to be granted official status, the Lightning had to be identical to what could be purchased at any Ford SVT dealer. The only external modifications allowed was the folding in of the side mirrors and the removal of the radio antenna. The speed of the truck was to be measured over one kilometer (approximately 0.62 miles), and the record speed was the average of speeds in both directions. Timing lights were set up seven-tenths of a mile apart (as certified by an independent surveyor) and a "Hot Lap In-Car Timer" from Longacre Racing Products was used to measure elapsed time through the measured 0.7 mile. Elapsed time was then converted to miles per hour. Clockwise, the Lightning's fastest elapsed time was 17.03 seconds, or 147.974mph. Counter-clockwise, its fastest time was 17.09 seconds, or 147.454mph, for an average of 147.714mph.

The Lightning's driver, Tom Chapman, Ford SVT chassis systems supervisor, offered a professional assessment of the Lightning's high speed achievement: "This may seem like fun and games, but high-speed stability is critical for a performance vehicle, even a pickup truck. The SVT F-150 Lightning is just as stable and planted at 147mph as it is at 55mph; only the scenery's going by faster. That stability is a testament to the solid foundation of the Ford F-150, and the performance engineering found in Ford SVT products".

Tom Scarpello was equally enthusiastic about the Lightning's

From top: John Coletti, chief engineer at Ford Special Vehicle Engineering introducing the 2001 F-150SVT Lightning at the SEMA show in Las Vegas, Nevada, October 31, 2001; The 2001 F-150 Lightning; A view of the 2001 Lightning displaying its side exhausts, lowered profile, 18in wheels and low profile tires. (Courtesy of SVT Media Services)

success: "We're proud to have certification from Guiness World Records. It is a well-deserved record for the engineering team and overdue confirmation to all the SVT F-150 Lightning owners out there who have known for years that they drive the fastest truck on the planet! Capable of acceleration from 0-60mph in 5.2 seconds and reaching 147mph, the SVT Lightning is the dominant sport pickup in the world. No pickup truck on the market today can come close to matching these numbers. And the SVT Lightning does all this and can still tow a 5000 pound trailer and carry 1300 pounds of payload. But best of all, this is no concept vehicle - it's available right now from your local Ford SVT dealer".

With sales of 840,586 for 2003, the F-150 pickup was once again the top-selling vehicle in the US.

75

The 2001 F-150 Lightning wasn't a sports car, but it cornered in a tight and taut fashion. (Courtesy of SVT Media Services)

The 2001 SVT Lightning's clear fog lamps and deep 'chin' spoiler contributed to its imposing appearance. (Courtesy of SVT Media Services)

F-150 model and option prices (2003)

Model	MSRP*
XL Styleside	
2WD Reg. Cab, short bed	$18,715
2WD Reg. Cab, long bed	$19,015
4WD Reg. Cab, short bed	$22,055
4WD Reg. Cab, long bed	$22,355
2WD SuperCab, short bed	$21,365
2WD SuperCab, long bed	$21,665
4WD SuperCab, short bed	$25,230
4WD SuperCab, long bed	$25,530
XL Flareside	
2WD Reg. Cab, short bed	$19,725
4WD Reg. Cab, short bed	$23,065
2WD SuperCab, short bed	$22,375
4WD SuperCab, short bed	$26,240
XLT Styleside	
2WD Reg. Cab, short bed	$21,185
2WD Reg. Cab, long bed	$21,480
4WD Reg. Cab, short bed	$24,600
4WD Reg. Cab, long bed	$24,910
2WD SuperCab, ext. cab, short bed	$24,030
2WD SuperCab, ext. cab, long bed	$24,330
4WD SuperCab, ext. cab, short bed	$27,840
4WD SuperCab, ext. cab, long bed	$28,140
2WD SuperCrew, crew cab, short bed	$27,875
4WD SuperCrew, crew cab, short bed	$31,090
XLT Flareside	
2WD Reg. Cab, short bed	$22,195
4WD Reg Cab, short bed	$25,610
2WD SuperCab, ext. cab, short bed	$25,040
4WD SuperCab, ext. bed, short bed	$28,855

continued next page

Model	MSRP*
Lariat Styleside	
2WD SuperCab, ext. cab, short bed	$27,500
2WD SuperCab, ext. cab, long bed	$27,800
2WD SuperCrew, crew cab, short bed	$29,865
4WD SuperCrew, crew cab, short bed	$33,320
Lariat Flareside	
2WD SuperCab, ext. cab, short cab	$28,510
4WD SuperCab, ext. cab, short bed	$30,795
4WD SuperCab, ext. cab, long bed	$31,095
4WD SuperCab, ext. cab, short bed	$31,805
King Ranch Flareside	
2WD SuperCab, ext. cab, short bed	$31,310
4WD SuperCab, ext. cab, short bed	$34,605
King Ranch Styleside	
2WD SuperCrew, crew cab, short bed	$32,765
4WD SuperCrew, crew cab, short bed	$36,220
Lightning Flareside	
2WD Reg. Cab, short bed	$32,515
Harley-Davidson Styleside	
2WD SuperCrew, crew cab, short bed	$36,555

Ford claimed a 0-60mph time for the 2001 Lightning of 5.8 seconds. (Courtesy of SVT Media Services)

Regular Cab SWB — Styleside
119.9" WB 4x2
120.2" WB 4x4

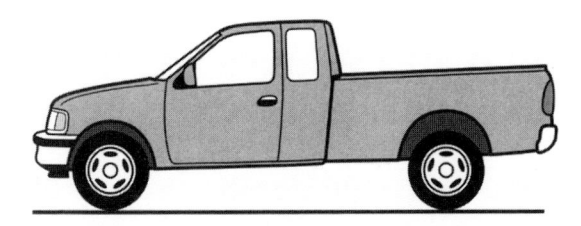

SuperCab SWB — Styleside
138.5" WB 4x2
138.8" WB 4x4

Regular Cab SWB — Flareside
119.9" WB 4x2
120.2" WB 4x4

SuperCab SWB — Flareside
138.5" WB 4x2
138.8" WB 4x4

Regular Cab LWB — Styleside
138.5" WB 4x2
138.8" WB 4x4

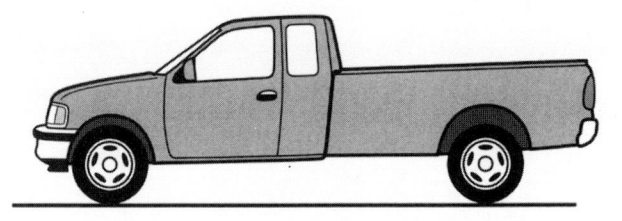

SuperCab LWB — Styleside
157.1" WB 4x2
157.4" WB 4x4

F-150 SuperCrew
138.5" WB 4x2
138.8" WB 4x4

The 2002 F-150 was available in these seven configurations. (Author's collection)

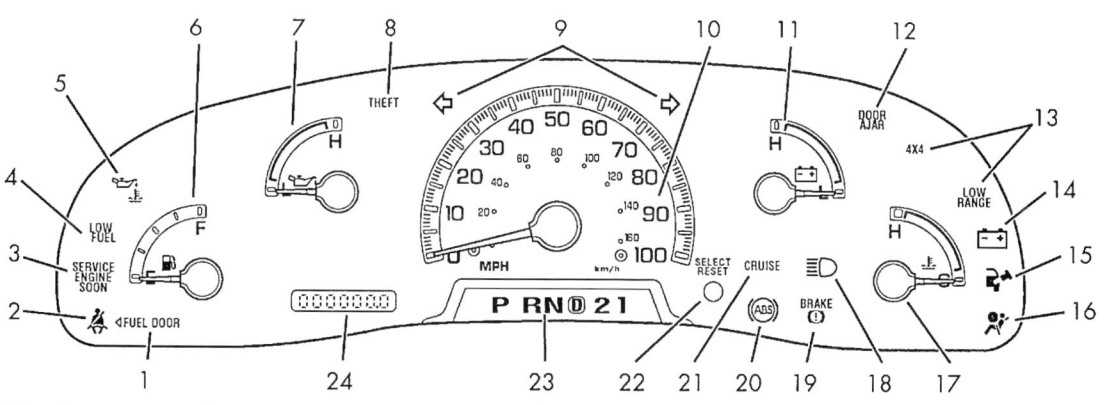

1. Fuel door location reminder
2. Fasten safety belt warning light
3. Service engine soon warning light
4. Low fuel warning light
5. Oil pressure/engine coolant temperature warning light
6. Fuel gauge
7. Engine oil pressure gauge
8. SecuriLock™ passive anti-theft system warning light
9. Turn signal indicators
10. Speedometer
11. Voltmeter
12. Door ajar warning light
13. 4x4 system indicator lights[1]
14. Charging system warning light
15. Check fuel cap warning light
16. Airbag readiness indicator/ warning light
17. Engine coolant temperature gauge
18. High-beam indicator light
19. Brake system warning light/ parking brake
20. Anti-lock Braking System warning light
21. Speed control indicator light
22. Trip odometer select/reset button
23. Automatic transmission gearshift indicator[1]
24. Odometer/trip odometer

Details of the 2002 XL F-150 instrument cluster. (Author's collection)

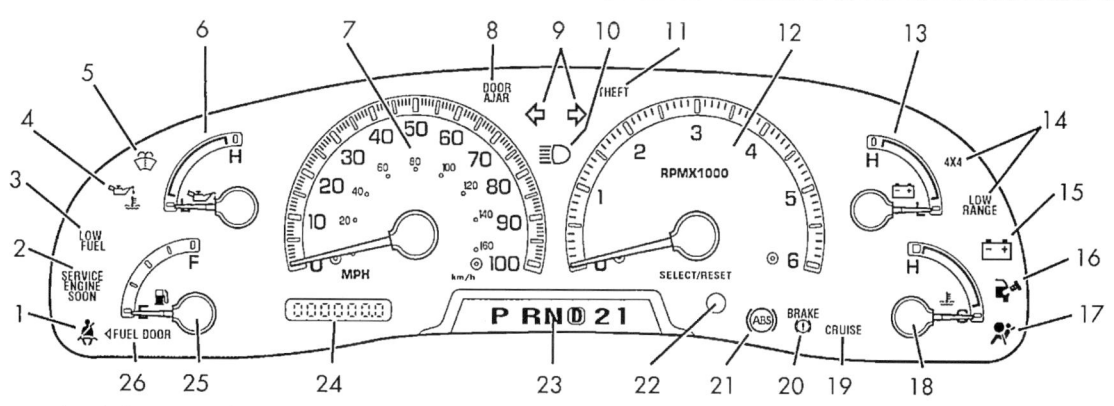

1. Fasten safety belt warning light
2. Service engine soon warning light
3. Low fuel warning light
4. Oil pressure/engine coolant temperature warning light
5. Low windshield washer fluid light
6. Engine oil pressure gauge
7. Speedometer
8. Door ajar warning light
9. Turn signal indicators
10. High-beam indicator light
11. SecuriLock™ passive anti-theft system warning light
12. Tachometer
13. Voltmeter
14. 4x4 system indicator lights[1]
15. Charging system warning light
16. Check fuel cap warning light
17. Airbag readiness indicator/ warning light
18. Engine coolant temperature gauge
19. Speed control indicator light
20. Brake system warning light/ parking brake
21. Anti-lock Braking System warning light
22. Trip odometer/select/reset button
23. Automatic transmission gearshift indicator[1]
24. Odometer/trip odometer
25. Fuel gauge
26. Fuel door location reminder

(1) If equipped.

The XLT and Lariat for 2002 shared this instrument cluster arrangement. (Author's collection)

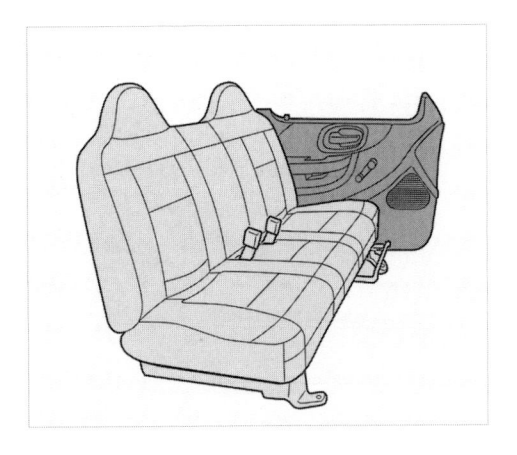

The 2002 XL bench seat. A cloth version in Dark Graphite or Medium Parchment was standard. As an option, Dark Graphite vinyl upholstery was available. It was included in the Work Truck Group. (Author's collection)

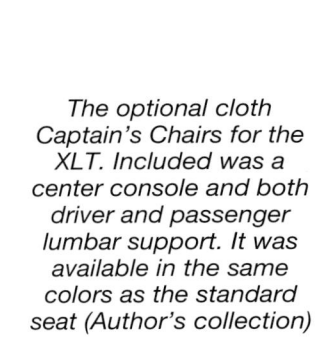

The optional cloth Captain's Chairs for the XLT. Included was a center console and both driver and passenger lumbar support. It was available in the same colors as the standard seat (Author's collection)

The 2002 XLT Regular Cab F-150's standard cloth 40/60 split bench seat. Both driver and passenger lumbar support was included. It was optional for the XL. Available colors Medium Graphite, Medium Parchment, and Dark Graphite. (Author's collection)

The 2002 SuperCab version of the XLT's optional cloth Captain's Chairs. (Author's collection)

The 2002 XLT SuperCrew's optional cloth Captain's Chairs. (Author's collection)

80

The standard 2002 XLT cloth 60/40 split bench seat. It was offered in the three available interior colors. (Author's collection)

The 2002 Lariat SuperCrew was equipped with this split bench seat with driver and front passenger lumbar support. Both the front and rear seats had leather seating surfaces. Lariat seats were offered in Medium Graphite or Medium Parchment. (Author's collection)

The standard cloth XLT 40/60 split bench seat for the SuperCab. It was offered in the three available interior colors. (Author's collection)

The Lariat's optional Captain's Chairs with console and front and rear leather seating surfaces. (Author's collection)

2002 King Ranch SuperCrew had these quad Captain's Chairs. The SuperCab version had a rear bench seat. Both were finished in Medium Parchment cloth with Castano brown leather trim. The SuperCrew had front and rear consoles with King Ranch leather-covered lid/armrests and King Ranch logo. The rear console was not included with the SuperCab. The seat back and cushion of the driver and front passenger seats were heated. (Author's collection)

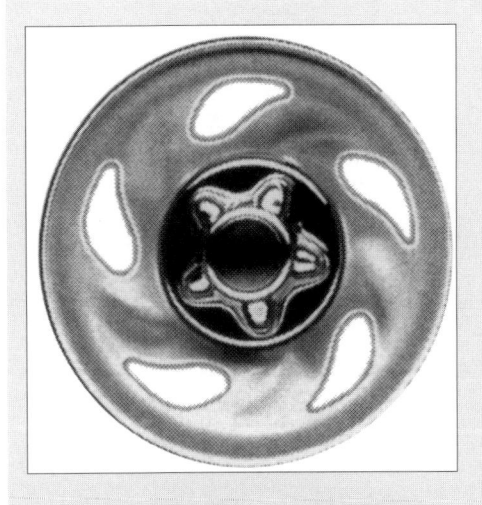

The standard XL wheel for 2002 was this 16 x 7in 5-lug Argent styled steel wheel with chrome center ornamentation. It was also used with the Work Truck Group with Argent center ornamentation. (Author's collection)

This 16 x 7in 7-lug Argent styled steel wheel was available only on 2002 XL and Work Group F-150 pickups with a Payload Group option. Chrome center ornamentation was used for the XL with an Argent center on the Work Truck. (Author's collection)

The standard F-150 Lariat wheel for 2002 was this 17 x 7.5in 5-lug chrome steel wheel with chrome center ornamentation. (Author's collection)

This 16 x 7in 5-lug 5-spoke cast aluminum wheel with chrome center was available only as an option for the 2002 XLT. (Author's collection)

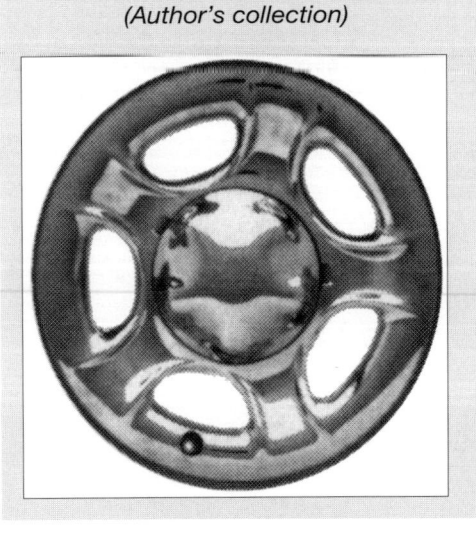

This 16 x 7in wheel was available only for 2002 XLT and Lariat F-150 pickups ordered with the 7700lb. Payload Group. (Author's collection)

82

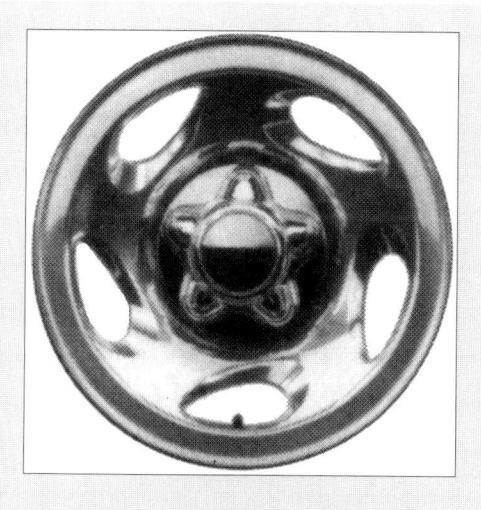

The standard XLT wheel for 2002. Also included in the Sport Group option for the XL, it was a 16 x 7in 5-lug polished aluminum wheel with a chrome center. (Author's collection)

A 17 x 7.5in 5-lug 5-spoke cast aluminum wheel with chrome center that was included only with the FX4 Off-Road Equipment Group for XLT and Lariat F-150 pickups. (Author's collection)

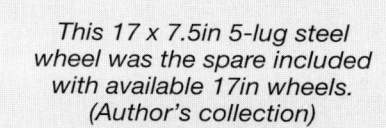

This 17 x 7.5in 5-lug steel wheel was the spare included with available 17in wheels. (Author's collection)

This 17 x 7.5in 5-lug 10-spoke cast aluminum wheel with a chrome center was included with the Sport Group option for the 2002 F-150 Lariat. It was also used, with painted spokes, for the King Ranch F-150. (Author's collection)

83

84

Opposite: Front and rear views of the 2001 F-150 Lariat SuperCab with a Bright Red/Arizona Beige color paint combination. (Courtesy of Ford Media Services)

The interior of a 2002 4x4 F-150 Lariat SuperCab in Medium Parchment. A loose fuel cap warning lamp was added to the instrument cluster for 2002. (Courtesy of Ford Media Services)

www.velocebooks.com/www.veloce.co.uk
All books in print • New books • Special offers • Newsletter

A detail view of the 2002 F-150 Harley-Davidson's grille insert. (Courtesy of Ford Media Services)

Below and oppsosite: Two views of the 2002 Harley-Davidson F-150. (Courtesy of Ford Media Services)

The 2002 F-150 Harley-Davidson's 20in chromed aluminum wheels were the same as those used in 2001. (Courtesy of Ford Media Services)

The 2002 Harley-Davidson F-150's quad Captain's Chairs with their black leather trim and Harley-Davidson badges were carried over from 2001. (Courtesy of Ford Media Services)

The new badging of the 2002 Harley-Davidson F-150 was positioned on its front fenders and tailgate. (Courtesy of Ford Media Services)

Above and opposite: These action shots of a 2002 Harley-Davidson F-150 on its own and keeping pace with a Harley-Davidson motorcycle, support Ford's assertion that it "flaunts a bold black-and-chrome theme, Harley-Davidson badging and 'In Your Face' performance". (Courtesy of Ford Media Services)

Powering the 2002 Harley-Davidson F-150 was a very mildly detuned version of the Lightning's supercharged 5.4 liter V-8. (Courtesy of Ford Media Services)

A 2003 F-150 XLT Styleside CrewCab. (Courtesy of Ford Media Services)

This 2003 F-150 XLT CrewCab was equipped with the optional bed extender and moonroof. On both the XLT and Lariat, the tailgate could be locked. (Courtesy of Ford Media Services)

A 2003 F-150 Lariat Flareside 4x4. A Group III Towing Group option for the F-150 included a 7-pin trailer wiring harness, frame mounted hitch receiver, heavy-duty electrical/cooling package, and heavy-duty shock absorbers. (Courtesy of Ford Media Services)

The 2003 F-150 Lariat dash panel. The leather-wrapped tilt steering wheel, speed control and AM/FM CD were standard. (Courtesy of Ford Media Services)

Power mirrors were standard for the F-150 Lariat. This is a view of the driver's side mirror of a 2003 F-150 Lariat. (Courtesy of Ford Media Services)

The interior of a 2003 F-150 XLT equipped with optional Captain's Chairs. (Courtesy of Ford Media Services)

The XL F-150 pickup had this exterior badging for 2003. (Courtesy of Ford Media Services)

An evocative view of a 2003 F-150 arriving at a country get-away for a weekend of open air activities. (Courtesy of Ford Media Services)

If powered by a Triton V-8, the 2003 XLT F-150 pickup had this front fender and tailgate identification. (Courtesy of Ford Media Services)

A perspective of the 5.4 liter Triton V-8 engine cover used for the 2003 model year. (Courtesy of Ford Media Services)

The optional 5.4 liter Triton V-8. This engine began the 2003 model having been named one of Ward's AutoWorld magazine's "Ten Best Engines" for six consecutive years. (Courtesy of Ford Media Services)

A 2003 F-150 SuperCrew equipped with an optional power moonroof. This pickup has the Bright Red/Shadow Grey color combination. (Courtesy of Ford Media Services)

This view shows the skid plate for the transfer case included in the 2003 FX4 option. (Courtesy of Ford Media Services)

A 2003 F-150 4x4 XLT SuperCab equipped with the FX4 Off-Road Equipment Group option. (Courtesy of Ford Media Services)

The interior of the 2003 F-150 King Ranch. The rear center console is in its stowed position. (Courtesy of Ford Media Services)

Identification for the 2003 F-150 King Ranch was unchanged from that used in previous years. (Courtesy of Ford Media Services)

The control for the 2003 F-150 King Ranch's standard heater front seats. (Courtesy of Ford Media Services)

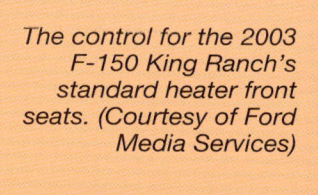

The 2003 F-150 King Ranch was equipped with this standard AM/FM/6-disc CD changer. (Courtesy of Ford Media Services)

The 2003 Ford F-150 Harley-Davidson SuperCrew in monochromatic Black. The front valance with built-in fog lamps was new for 2003. (Courtesy of Ford Media Services)

This new optional Black over Silver paint combination was available for the 2003 Ford Harley-Davidson F-150 SuperCrew. (Courtesy of Ford Media Services)

This "100th Anniversary" nameplate was positioned on the 2003 model's front fenders and tailgate. (Courtesy of Ford Media Services)

The "100th Anniversary" nameplate was also located on the 2003 Ford Harley-Davidson's console lid. (Courtesy of Ford Media Services)

101

A 2003 F-150 equipped with the new STX Package. This option's clear head and parking lamps, round fog lamps and chrome tubular step bars are apparent in this perspective. (Courtesy of Ford Media Services)

F-150s with 4wd and the STX package had this badging on the rear fender. Only the "STX" identification was used for 2wd models. (Courtesy of Ford Media Services)

A closeup view of the 17in five-spoke Chromtec wheels included in the 2003 F-150 STX package. This is an XLT model. (Courtesy of Ford Media Services)

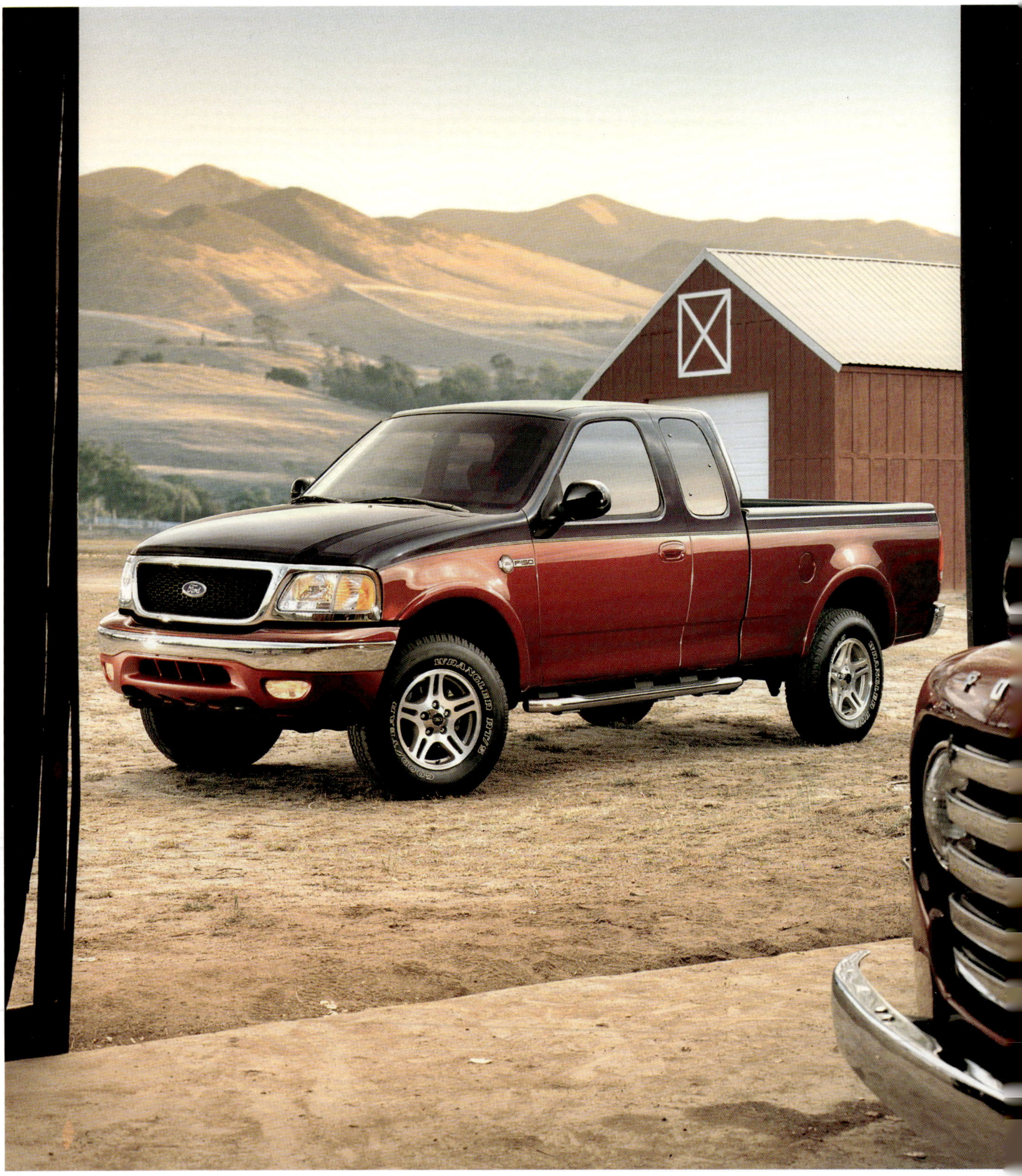

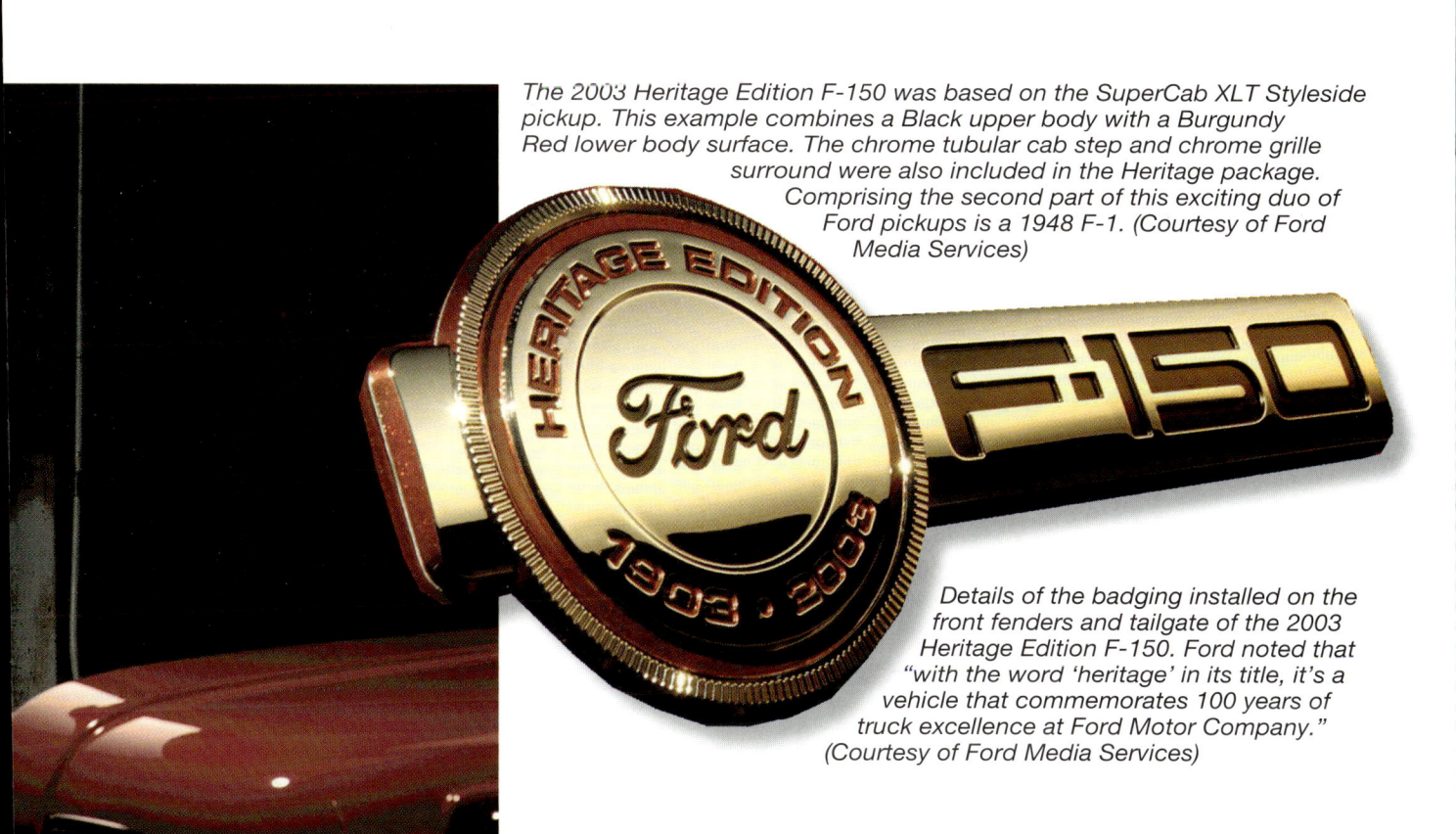

The 2003 Heritage Edition F-150 was based on the SuperCab XLT Styleside pickup. This example combines a Black upper body with a Burgundy Red lower body surface. The chrome tubular cab step and chrome grille surround were also included in the Heritage package. Comprising the second part of this exciting duo of Ford pickups is a 1948 F-1. (Courtesy of Ford Media Services)

Details of the badging installed on the front fenders and tailgate of the 2003 Heritage Edition F-150. Ford noted that "with the word 'heritage' in its title, it's a vehicle that commemorates 100 years of truck excellence at Ford Motor Company." (Courtesy of Ford Media Services)

On August 13, 2003, a 2003 SVT Lightning averaged 147.714mph at Ford's Michigan Proving Grounds to earn certification by Guinness World Records, Ltd. as the "World's Fastest Production Pickup Truck". (Courtesy of SVT Media Services)

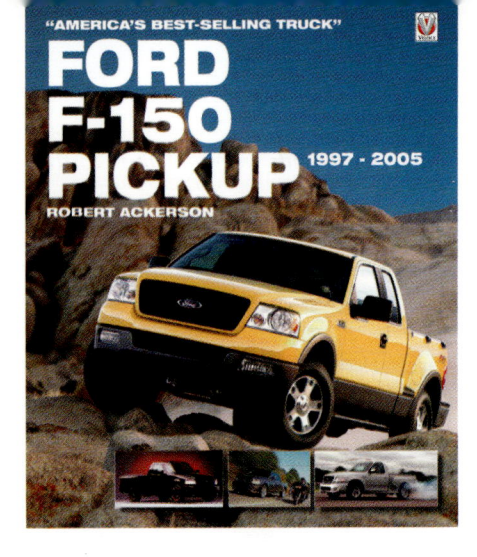

4
2004-2005

The 2004 Ford F-150 was introduced on January 6, 2004 with an all-new design intended to exceed the parameters of its predecessor in virtually every area of importance to full-size truck buyers. More 'Ford Tough' than ever, with increased interior room, and enhanced safety features, it was available with a new V-8 engine with more horsepower and torque and improved fuel economy than its 2003 counterpart.

Chris Theodore, Ford's vice president of North American Product Development offered this perspective of the new F-150's origins: "Our vision was to forge a new direction for the market, building on Ford's Tough Truck heritage and creating a product that would alter the expectations of pickup customers. The new F-150 does that with the courage of a leader, launching a new era of Built Ford Tough".

Ford's research of customer preferences in full-size pickups resulted in the availability of the 2004 F-150 in five distinct series: XL, STX, XLT, FX4, and the top-of the line Lariat. This 'segment differentiation' was the key to Ford's approach to the diverse nature of the full-size pickup truck market in the US.

Referring to this alignment, Doug Scott, Ford Division truck group marketing manager explained, "In essence, we are reinventing the rules in the full-size pickup market. We built on our heritage, listened to customer feedback, and developed a totally new approach that allows us to appeal to the full-size truck market and provide individualized versatility and character."

Three cab choices were available, all with four doors. The Regular Cab provided a single row of occupant seating and rearward-swinging access doors opening to a behind-seat, 13in wide, stowage area.

The SuperCab was a two-door extended cab version with a second row of seating accessed by an industry-first rearward-swinging access doors. When extended cab models were introduced in the 1990s, they accounted for less than 20 per cent of the total market. By the start of the 2004 model year, they represented approximately 80 per cent of pickup truck sales.

The Regular Cab and SuperCab passenger compartment was six inches longer than the previous models. The behind-seat cargo area was large enough to accommodate payload as

This page and opposite: The 2004 F-150 made its debut at the North American Auto Show in Detroit, Michigan on January 6, 2003. In these two photos, Steve Lyons, Vice President, Ford Division, Ford Motor Company, introduces the F-150 FX4. (Courtesy of Ford Media Services)

diverse as golf clubs, toolboxes, or five-gallon paint cans. Each access door had an integral window. On the XLT, FX4, and SuperCab models rear door power windows were standard. A power sliding rear window was optional.

Three bed lengths were offered: 8 foot, 6½ foot, and 5½ foot. All boxes were two inches deeper than in 2003, significantly increasing usable volume. The total cargo space of the 6½ foot box, for example, was 65 cubic feet, nearly 12 per cent more than that of the equivalent 2003 model. The Styleside box was available in all three box lengths. Flaresides were available only with a new 6½ box formed of inner steel panels and sheet molded composite exterior panels. Ford reported that "the stylish Flareside harks back to historic Ford models with deeper, fender-like wheel flares and a unique tailgate design that flares outward at its upper edge for a 'spoiler effect'". A new addition, and a full-size pickup truck exclusive, was the F-150 SuperCab with the 5½ foot bed. The tailgates for both box designs incorporated a new 'Tailgate Assist' with an internal torsion bar that reduced opening and closing effort.

Ford was not reluctant to admit that the chiseled lines of Ford's 'Mighty F-350 Tonka' concept truck had offered a preview of Ford's intentions for the styling of the 2004 F-150: "It's bold. It's strong. It's a hint of what's to come for the next generation Ford F-series pickup."

When he took the wraps off the Tonka at the 2002 North American International Auto Show in Detroit on January 6, 2002, James Padilla, group vice president, Ford North America, remarked that "It's as spirited as it is rugged, a blend you're likely to see on Ford trucks down the road."

J. Mays, vice president, Design, Ford Motor Company, added this teaser remark: "This truck is unmistakably a Ford and signals the direction we will take Tough Truck design in the future."

Against this background, Patrick Schiavone, Ford truck design director, outlined some of his team's objectives and challenges in designing a successor to the 2003 F-150: "Creating an all-new F-150 was about asserting the toughness and truck capability of the leader. We definitely wanted to push the design to a new level, to move the excitement needle up a notch. The result is a shape symbolic of strength with an underlying tone of sophistication that really gives this truck aspirational qualities."

Key elements of the F-150's new look were wider, by 1.5 inches, front and rear tracks, larger standard wheel and tire combinations, and circular wheel arches. Collectively, said Ford, these gave the F-150 a profile that was 'self-assured' and one that 'visually' communicates power. The front end had a new wrap-around fascia and quad-circle headlamps positioned in 'form-follows-function' clusters. The bumper accommodated integral fog lamps, if specified, and, on 4x4 models, tow hooks. The use of a high belt line emphasized the body's chiseled lines and what Ford depicted as "a roof line reminiscent

On January 6, 2002, Ford Media said this about the Mighty F-350 Tonka Concept: "It's bold. It's strong. It's a hint of what's to come for the next generation Ford F-Series pickup ..." (Courtesy of Ford Media Services)

Below: Chrome was applied generously to the F-350 TONKA, extending to the fender, deployable running boards, 22in wheels, door handles, and tow hooks. (Courtesy of Ford Media Services)

Bottom: The F-350 TONKA's front end was dominated by a massive sharply defined chrome grille and side "nostrils". (Courtesy of Ford Media Services)

of chopped-top custom street trucks". To balance the lower body's 'visual weight' that resulted, the side windows' inward bow, known as the tumblehome, was more perpendicular than on the previous model. This also allowed the use of nearly vertical flush side windows.

The F-150 interior, wider and roomier than in 2003, provided improved occupant comfort, reduced interior noise and additional feature content. "Truck owners spend more time than ever before in their vehicles", said Jim Smithbanner, F-150 design manager. "We designed the new F-150 interior to give them the comfort, craftsmanship, versatility, and features they want and deserve. The look is very modern, precise, and industrial, and it's executed in an honest, straightforward way."

Ford designed the cabin to accommodate the so-called 25th per centile woman (approximately 4ft 10in tall) and the 99th per centile man (approximately 6ft 4in tall). The door armrests extended far enough to please both large and small drivers. Grab handles were also placed within the range of virtually all occupants. Moving the optional running boards lower and farther outboard made them more useful for stepping up into the cab.

Great strides were made in cabin

The F-350 Tonka was depicted by Ford as "a brawny vehicle true to its 'Built Ford Tough' heritage. Its striking yellow hue, a tribute to the traditional TONKA pallette, is as eye-catching as its impressive size and distinctive styling". (Courtesy of Ford Media Services)

noise reduction. Liquid-filled engine mounts, dubbed 'hydromounts', diminished most of the engine's noise and vibration before it reached the passenger compartment. Also used to subdue interior noise were new inset doors with new double door seals, thicker front side windows, a laminated dash panel, and noise-blocking air extractor vents at the rear of the cab.

The benefits were noticeable. The F-150 cabin had highway cruise noise levels that were two sones quieter than the previous best-in-class standard. Similarly, on rough country-type roads (at more moderate speeds), the F-150's overall sound levels were 2.8dBA lower than the previous leader's. During wide-open throttle acceleration, the F-150's 'speech articulation index' - a measure of how easily a conversation can take place - was, at 3500rpm, five per cent lower than Ford's nearest competitor's.

The two-tone instrument panel was structured as a modular unit. Its vertical band format made possible combinations of different colors, textures, and materials, creating

The F-350 TONKA's chiseled lines and sheer surfaces are evident in this view. (Courtesy of Ford Media Services)

Bill Ford, Ford Motor Company chairman and CEO, accompanied by Gerald Bantam, vice-president, United Auto Workers, drives the first 2004 F-150 off the assembly line at Ford's Norfork, VA plant. on January 10, 2003. (Courtesy of Ford Media Services)

customized appearances. Three different instrument cluster designs were also offered, along with other elements to give each series a distinctive look.

Thanks to their new flow-through center console, FX4 and Lariat models could be equipped with optional dual Captain's Chairs and a steel and chrome floor shifter. Pickups with the standard 40/20/20 split-frontbench seat had a different instrument panel center stack to optimize middle passenger leg room.

A new brushed aluminum modular overhead rail system was standard on XLT, FX4, and Lariat SuperCab and SuperCrew models, allowing customers to select suitable interior storage options. This item, with an integral power supply, was incorporated into the headliner and extended from the rearview mirror to just aft of the second row of seats. The rail's forward end contained a dome light console and a large storage bin module. Owners could easily snap in additional modules such as first aid kits, toolboxes, flashlights, and two-way radios as they were offered by both Ford and after market suppliers. At the start of the model year an optional rear seat DVD entertainment system was available for the XLT, FX4, and Lariat SuperCrew trucks.

Ford described the F-150 XL as exemplifying "the pickup's role in building America. It is the workhorse truck that gets the job done, and can get down and get dirty with hose-out floor functionality". The XL was available in both Regular Cab and SuperCab models with a choice of vinyl or cloth interior. The regular cab configuration was equipped with the new rear access doors opening to the stowage area behind the truck's 40/20/20 split-bench seat.

The XL had standard 17in steel wheels. New features included a standard tilt steering wheel and a center display system in the instrument panel.

The F-150 STX combined the work truck capabilities of the XL with many sporty features. It was available in Regular Cab or SuperCab body styles and had body-color bumpers and 17in cast aluminum wheels. A Styleside 6½ foot box was standard, with a Flareside box optional. The SuperCab version was available with an optional 5½ foot Styleside box. An extra-cost 'audiophile' sound system consisted of an AM/FM radio and 6-disc CD changer with sub woofer. The standard engine for both the STX and XL was the 4.6 liter Triton V-8.

The F-150 XLT was available in all cab variations and, depending on the cab, with all Styleside box lengths and Flareside configurations. The XLT had its own unique grille treatment and standard 17in cast aluminum wheels. Fog lamps were standard on 4x4 models. A Silver two-tone finish was optional.

Standard interior appointments included chrome instrument panel accents, premium cloth for the 40/20/20 split-bench seat, and the new overhead rail system. SuperCab and SuperCrew models had standard second-row power windows. Other standard XLT equipment included power mirrors, autolamp, delayed accessory power, outside temperature/compass display, and speed control. Optional equipment included a defrosting rear window, fog lamps on 4x2 models, a keyless entry door keypad, and, for the SuperCab and SuperCrew, a power moon roof.

Ford depicted the FX4 as "aimed at outdoor enthusiasts who believe 4-wheel drive capability is a critical lifestyle elements". FX4 models were available in Regular Cab, SuperCab and SuperCrew body styles. Depending on cab choice, box configurations consisted of 6½ foot Styleside, 6½ foot Flareside, or the 5½ foot Styleside.

Body-color bumpers and a unique grille highlighted the FX4 exterior. Machined aluminum 17in wheels were standard. Machined cast 18in aluminum wheels were optional as was a new Dark Shadow Gray lower two-tone exterior paint treatment.

The focus of the FX4 interior was an instrument panel with 'carbon mesh accents and chrome-ringed air registers intended to evoke images of classic aviation. The steering wheel was leather-wrapped. The standard cloth 40/20/20 bench seat could be replaced by optional Captain's Chairs with either cloth or leather upholstery. Accompanying these seats was the flow-through center console, and floor shifter. For serious off-road use, the F-150 FX4 was equipped with skid plates, heavy-duty shock absorbers, and a standard limited-slip 3.73:1 rear axle. LT tires were optional.

The top-of-the line Lariat was geared, said Ford, "to buyers who view their trucks as a reward for achievement". Ford research indicated that Lariat owners used their trucks for a wide range of functions; from everyday driving to towing boats and travel trailers.

The Lariat's primary exterior features were its 18in bright aluminum wheels, chrome bumpers, unique grille, and optional Arizona Beige lower two-tone paint treatment. The Lariat's standard 40/20/20 leather split bench seat could be replaced by optional premium heated dual power leather Captain's Chairs accompanied by the new flow-through console and floor shifter. Both the instrument panel and center console contained stitched surfaces in Medium Pebble or Ebony. Woodgrain accents were positioned on the doors and the instrument panel center stack.

Chrome-rings surrounding the instrument cluster's cream-colored gauges matched other chromed interior items, including the door handles and round air registers. The steering wheel had built-in controls for key audio and climate control functions. Additional special Lariat features included an in-dash message center, electronic automatic temperature control, and power-adjustable memory seats and pedals. The Lariat's heated side mirrors had built-in repeater lamps synchronized with the turn signals.

Beneath the new F-150 exterior was a newly engineered frame and body structure. Along with virtually all aspects of the new F-150, they had been developed with the aid of C3P, Ford's computer-aided 'tool set'.

C3P was an integrated package of computer-aided design, computer-aided engineering, computer-aided manufacturing, and a comprehensive product information base that allowed designers and engineers to create the new F-150 largely in a digital environment. As a result, Ford engineers were able to reduce the number of hard prototypes needed during the engineering process to test new component designs. In place of these vehicles, engineers built virtual prototypes of digital designs and test them in the digital environment. This significantly cut time from the development process, allowing engineering resources to be concentrated on optimizing functionality rather than on testing a succession of prototypes as done in the past.

"We were exploring thousands of design options at once", explained Anthony Selley, F-150 chassis supervisor. "The only way to do this is with computer-aided engineering. CAE allowed us to weigh all the options before we actually built the designs and subjected them to instrumented testing."

During desing three-dimensional digital representations of the frame, power train, suspension, and body were run through deflection simulations that exaggerated actual movements by a factor of 50. The frame was fully-boxed with hydroformed front rails to form a closed section as opposed to the traditional 'C' rail design. Critical cross members were welded to the rails with what Ford called a

Bill Ford and Gerald Bantam celebrating the production of the first 2004 F-150. (Courtesy of Ford Media Services)

Virginia Governor Mark Warner congratulating Bill Ford on Ford's centennial and the first 2004 F-150 produced at Norfolk. (Courtesy of Ford Media Services)

Bill Ford was all smiles when the first 2004 F-150 was completed in June, 2003. The 5.4 liter Triton V-8 that powered this truck was the 100 millionth V-8 produced by the Ford Motor Company. (Courtesy of Ford Media Services)

'through-rail' joint to prevent localized flex. Large 'wide-footprint' brackets attached the suspension, body, and power train to the frame. The entire frame was welded together and was approximately nine times stiffer in torsion and 50 per cent stiffer than the 2003 model's.

The new body structure was approximately 75 per cent stiffer than that of the 2003 truck. This gain was achieved at the same time as the length of the Regular Cab and SuperCab models was extended by six inches and dual rear access doors were added to the Regular Cab.

A key contributor to this stiffness was the extensive use of a special structural adhesive joining the various stampings comprising the body's floor. Applied robotically for consistency and speed, the adhesive bonded the metal in spaces between spot welds, forming a continuous seam. This provided increased stiffness and reduced localized stresses at the weld points for increased durability. Additional improvements to the body stiffness were credited to the use of high-strength steel reinforcements at key areas such as the rocker panels and door openings.

Both the F-150's body and engine mounts were redesigned. These mounts were a crucial part of the truck's system, serving to isolate the passenger compartment from vibrations that reach the frame. The mounts on both sides of the passenger cabin had a new "shear" design utilizing two concentric tubes, one bolted to the frame, the other bolted to the body structure. Rubber was bonded between the two tubes. The metal tubes also improved passenger safety in a crash by limiting fore and aft movement of the

From left to right: 2004 F-150 XLT, STX, Lariat, and FX4. (Courtesy of Ford Media Services)

passenger compartment. The engine mounting location was reinforced to improve the ability of the hydraulic engine mounts to absorb power train vibrations before they reach the passenger compartment.

Double-sided galvanized steel was used for virtually all body panels. The roof was galvanized on one side only. A full phosphate dip plus 'High-Edge E-Coat' panels helped protect most body and chassis components. The front edges of the hood received a thicker coat of primer before painting. A clearcoat paint and a PVC coating were sprayed on the lower bodyside for additional chip and corrosion protection. The lower hem flanges on the doors were sealed with a special weather-resistant adhesive.

Both 4x2 and 4x4 models had front suspensions of an all-new coil spring over shock absorber design with cast-aluminum lower control arms, long-spindle double wishbone, and rate-plate bushings. Ford identified the suspension mounting points on the frame as having a 'large-footprint' design that provided a strong base for the suspension system.

The front track was increased by 1.6in to 67in. Mounting the shock absorber inside the coil spring permitted more precise suspension tuning and commonality across the F-150 line. The shock absorber was also moved closer to the wheel, increasing mechanical advantage by approximately 25 per cent.

The use of cast-aluminum, a first in the F-150's market segment, reduced unsprung mass; the parts of a vehicle that moves up and down as the suspension compresses and extends. The heavier a suspension component, the more likely it is to initially resist motion in response to a change in the road surface; and the longer it tends to remain in motion after the the truck has passed over the irregularity. The design of the lower control arms also provided a better ride and improved stability on choppy, broken surfaces. The new front bushings were soft in response to road impacts but stiff for cornering capability. Voids in key areas of the bushings let the rubber 'give' under pressure and allow the front wheels to momentarily move forward in response to a sharp jolt, resulting in a softer ride.

The ratio of lateral to longitudinal response of the aft lower control arm's bushings was 29:1, which was superior to that of many performance sedans. In a severe frontal impact, the lower suspension arms were designed to fracture, absorbing crash energy.

The front stabilizer bar was mounted in what Ford labeled 'gripping' bushings. This design kept the bushing compressed against the

Right and below: Two views of a 2004 F-150 FX4 introduced on stage just prior to the opening of a Toby Keith concert at Ford's Centennial Celebration held at its World Headquarters. (Courtesy of Ford Media Services)

stabilizer bar, allowing the bushing to twist with it. The bushing provided higher linear loading for 'crisper' steering response while having a relatively low rate for a smooth ride. The stabilizer bar had ball joints at each end to reduce compliance in the stabilizer bar system and improve response.

The new arrangement placed the brake deeper inside the wheel, which reduced scrub radius; the distance between the tire patch center and the steering pivot to 15mm. As recently as 2002 it had been 50mm. This reduced leverage from road forces on the steering pivot, which increased stability and steering control while braking.

The rear leaf springs were three inches wide, 20 per cent more than the 2003 F-150's and the same width as those used on Ford's Super Duty models. The rear suspension track was increased by 1.5in. Along with outboard-mounted shock absorbers, these changes provided increased roll damping and lateral stiffness for improved handling and a better ride. The positioning of the shock absorbers reduced the amount the truck leaned, particularly during situations such as lane changes. They also reduced the axle's tendency to 'skip and skate' on washboard type surfaces. The rear suspension was more resistant to side loads such as those generated by rutted roads, trailers in crosswinds, and when in close proximity to 18-wheelers.

Ford claimed that the F-150's new rack-and-pinion steering system was "the largest, strongest, and most rugged" it had ever used on a pickup. For the first time, two steering rack ratios were used, matched to the truck's wheelbase, contributing to

114

A 2004 F-150 FX4. Ford reported that the FX4 was designed to look at home in rugged terrain. (Courtesy of Ford Media Services)

a common steering feel across the model range. It was much stiffer than the recirculating-ball system used on the 2003 F-150 with less operating friction and lash for improved steering control and feedback. It also made for a relatively tight 46 foot turning circle for the SuperCab models. "You interact with the steering wheel for the entire time you are driving", said Dan Gompper, F-150 vehicle dynamics supervisor. "That interaction reveals more about the vehicle than anything else. The steering wheel of the F-150 immediately communicates the performance potential of the vehicle."

The F-150 was equipped with standard 4-wheel disc brakes, 4-wheel anti-lock control (ABS) and electronic brake force distribution (EBD), providing both improved braking performance and brake feel. Compared to the previous model's, the new system's rotors were larger and thicker, and the calipers were 60 per cent stiffer. The brake pads were made of high-friction semi-metallic lining material. The vented front discs had twin-piston calipers and were 13in in diameter, an increase of 0.87in from those of the 2003 model. The vented rear discs, with single-piston calipers had a diameter of 13.7in, an increase of 0.55in. These larger rotors provided more surface area for brake pad contact, more powerful braking and better heat dissipation for more consistent braking performance.

The EBD system managed the brake force between the front and rear wheels, helping to shorten braking distances and maximize the rear-wheel braking while the truck was used for towing. EBD used data measured by sensors to compare wheel speed more than 100 times during each rotation. If wheel lockup was imminent, the EBD controller was able to redirect brake force within milliseconds to optimize available traction.

The F-150's chassis and body were subjected to "an extensive corrosion resistance program" that included a 17-week test at Ford's Arizona Proving Ground. Key aspects included the 'Saltbath', 'Humidity Chamber', and the 'Drying Chamber'. Sixty cycles of this test were judged to be the equivalence of six years of operation in Canada's Maritime Provinces. The F-150 prototypes completed hundreds of cycles. Overall, the new F-150 test mileage was the equivalent of over five million miles of driving.

4-wheel drive models used either the current model's manual or electronic shift-on-the-fly transfer case. A selection of limited-slip rear

A cutaway view of The 2004 F-150's 5.4 liter Triton 3-valve V-8 showing elements of its variable cam timing and three-valve-per-cylinder design. (Courtesy of Ford Media Services)

The use of variable camshaft timing on the 2004 5.4 liter Triton V-8 allowed the valves to operate at different points in the combustion cycle, tailoring performance to the engine's specific speed and load at a given point. (Courtesy of Ford Media Services)

The 2004 F-150 frame. The front frame rails were hydroformed to enhance their ability to bear the load of the front suspension and powertrain. The full frame was also formed into a closed box section, strengthening the attachment points between the body and frame. The cross members were inserted through the side rails and welded on both sides. (Courtesy of Ford Media Services)

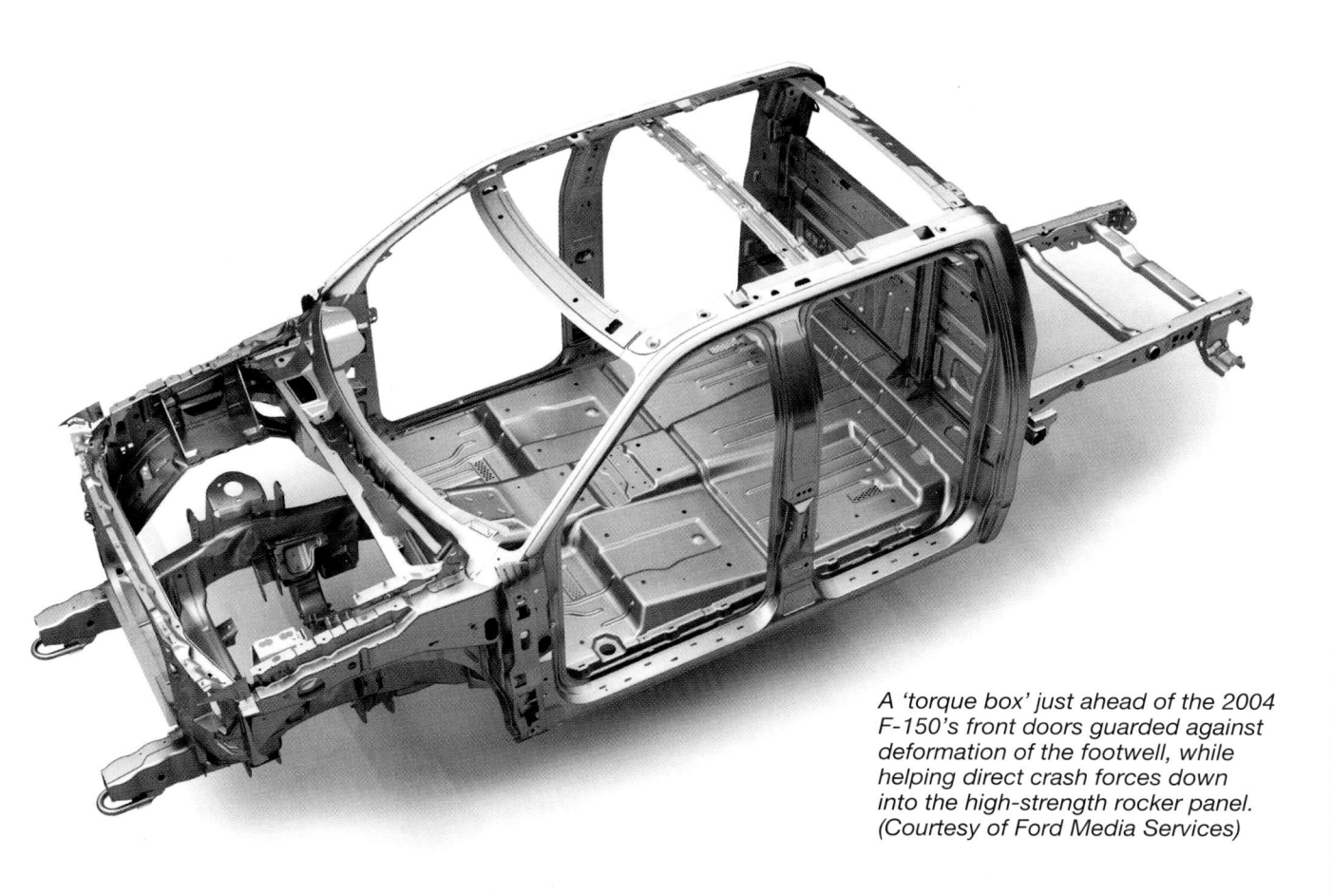

A view of the 5.4 liter Triton V-8's three-valve cylinder head and single overhead cam for each bank of cylinders. (Courtesy of Ford Media Services)

A 'torque box' just ahead of the 2004 F-150's front doors guarded against deformation of the footwell, while helping direct crash forces down into the high-strength rocker panel. (Courtesy of Ford Media Services)

The Charge Motion Control Valve flaps of the 5.4 liter Triton V-8 used computer-designed cutouts to induce turbulence in the air/fuel mixture at low engine speeds. (Courtesy of Ford Media Services)

Below: Safety enhancements were integrated into the 2004 F-150's passenger cabin. They included a new weight-saving front seat that helped tailor air bag response to specific situations. (Courtesy of Ford Media Services)

axles was optional. For off-road use, the 4x4 models had a new 4-Low throttle calibration and anti-lock brakes tuned for loose surfaces. The electronic throttle control incorporated a dedicated low-range acceleration response design for better control of torque in slippery conditions and reduced bucking when the truck crossed rough terrain.

The F-150's safety feature portfolio was identified as the Ford Personal Safety System. Included was a sensor mounted to the seat track that tailored the front air bag's inflation force to the severity of the crash, the driver's safety belt, and the driver's seat position. In addition, a new weight-sensing front passenger seat helped adapt air bag response to specific situations. If the sensor detected no weight on the front passenger seat - or very little weight - such as a newspaper, a half-dozen bagels, or work gloves - the passenger-side air bag was automatically turned off. If more weight was detected on the seat, as with a small child, the air bag remained turned off and a light on the instrument panel illuminated the message 'PASSENGER AIR BAG OFF'. If an adult occupied the passenger seat, the light was extinguished and the air bag was automatically switched on. To encourage safety belt use, the F-150 was fitted with Ford's BeltMinder system which prompted the driver and, for the first time in a truck, the front passenger to buckle up.

The F-150 was available with two Triton SOHC V-8 engine choices, the base 4.6 liter or the optional 5.4 liter. The latter V-8 was all-new with three valves (two intake, one exhaust valve per cylinder), variable cam timing, an all-new aluminum cylinder head, and an improved cast-iron block. With magnesium camshaft covers, this engine weighed no more than conventional two-valve V-8 engines.

The 3-valve heads were

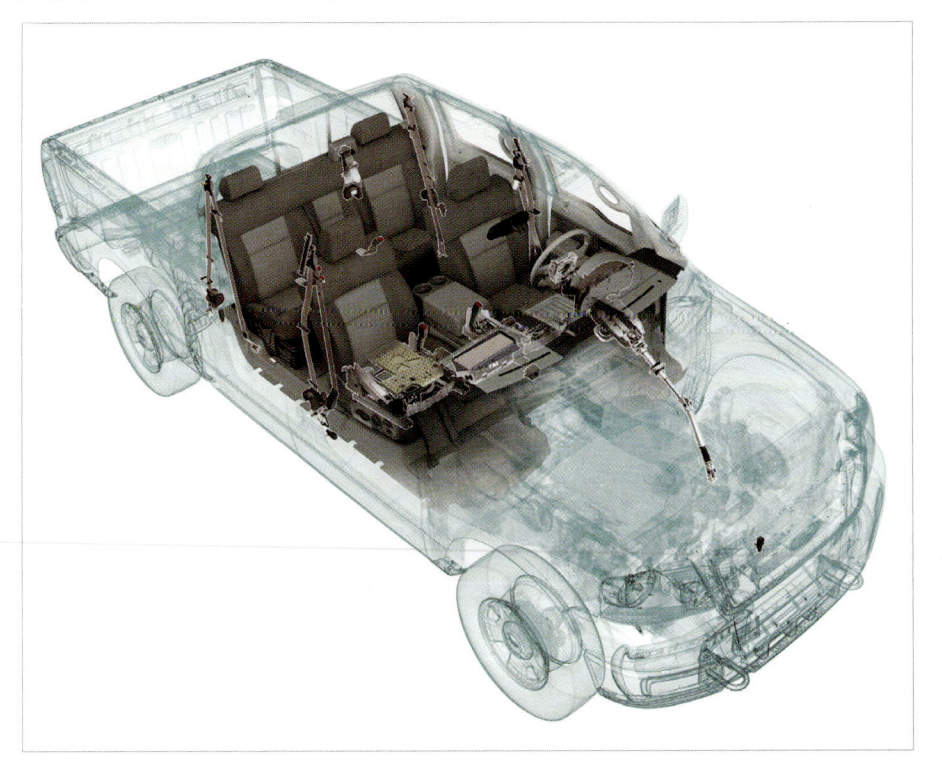

A 2004 F-150 STX SuperCab. (Courtesy of Ford Media Services)

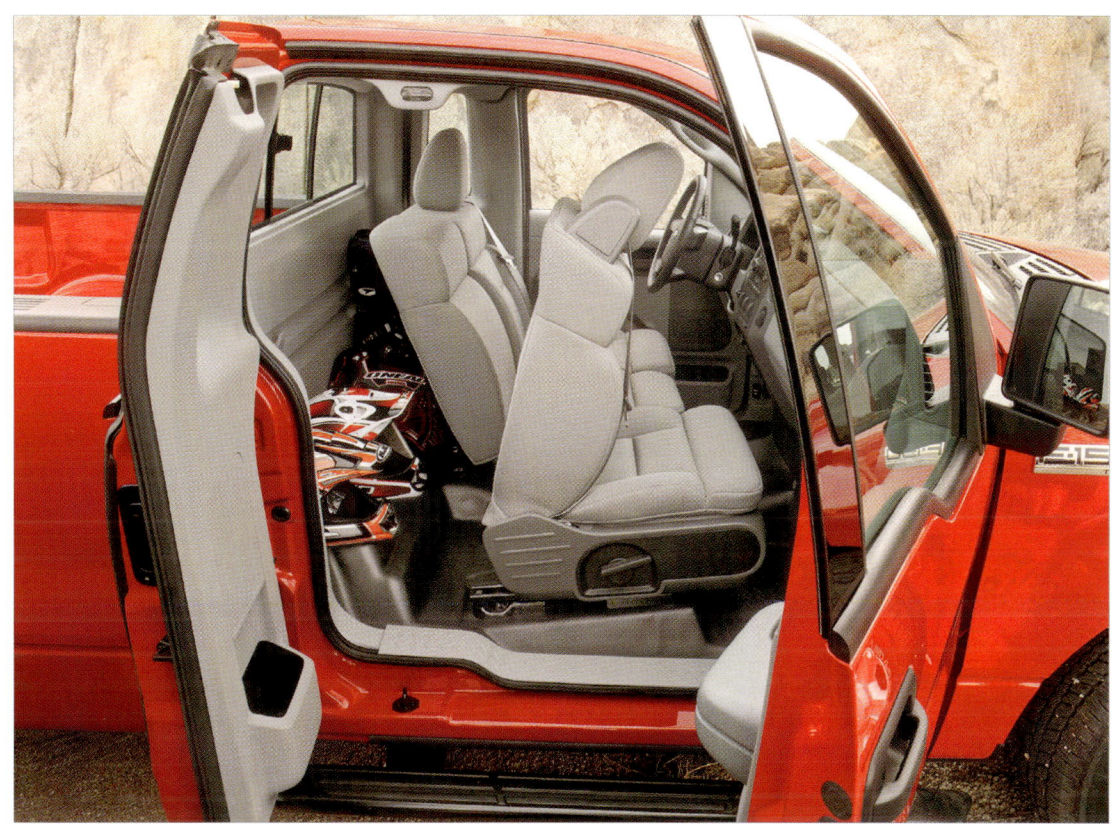

dimensionally smaller than the 2-valve design for the 5.4 liter V-8, while offering more rigidity and strength. It was also easier to manufacture. The 3-valve cylinder head was produced at Ford's Windsor, Ontario Engine Plant with the full engine assembled at the Essex Engine Plant, also located in Windsor. Both plants were past winners of the Shingo Award for Excellence in Manufacturing. Together they produced 1.1million V-6, V-8, and V-10 engines in 2001.

With 300hp@5000rpm, the 5.4 liter V-8 was 15 per cent more powerful than its predecessor, the 2-valve per cylinder Triton V-8 that had been named to *Wards'* 10 Best Engine list for six consecutive years. Peak torque was 365lb/ft@3750rpm. Both low-speed and high end torque output was improved, as was fuel economy.

This engine used dual equal-variable cam timing to simultaneously shift the intake and exhaust valve timing. This allowed the valves to be operated at different points in the combustion cycle, providing performance tailored to specific engine speed and load conditions. Ford predicted that the driver would not notice the cams were changing but would be able to sense the engine producing more power when needed, particularly at lower engine speeds, such as when the truck was being used for towing or heavy hauling.

This technology involved the use of electrically controlled Charge Motion Control Valves (CMCV) located in the intake runners. These were specially shaped to speed up the intake charge and induce a tumble effect in the combustion chamber at lower speeds and lighter loads. This caused the fuel to mix more thoroughly and to burn quickly and efficiently, with reduced emissions, particularly at idle.

The CMCV's were controlled by an electronic motor, and opened at a predetermined point as engine speed increased. At higher engine speeds the intake charge was unchanged, allowing undisturbed maximum flow into the combustion chambers at wide-open throttle.

The holistic approach Ford engineers adopted to the design of this engine resulted in advances in one area having a beneficial effect upon other aspect of the engine's operation. For example, while Ford's noise, vibration, and harshness (NVH) engineers used computer modeling to design vibration-resistant ribbing and reinforcement into the composite intake manifold, the design of the intake and exhaust manifolds providing better air flow and improve efficiency also resulted in quieter operation.

Since the engine was the main source of perceived noise levels by the truck's occupants, Ford engineers 'managed' engine sound by using sound-insulating materials and a three-part tuned mass absorber in the "valley" beneath the intake runners. In addition, a new sound-absorbing engine cover was used that wrapped around the edges of sound absorbing blankets at the engine's front and rear. At the top of the engine, new magnesium cam covers had the same vibration-resistance quality of aluminum covers but were weighed less. Cast into the covers were reinforcing ribs, which, along

Myren D. Strokes, publisher of EMOTION!REPORTS.com, presented Ford Division President Stephen Lyons with an award naming the 2004 F-150 the "Truck of the Decade", at the Chicago Auto Show on February 4, 2004. (Courtesy of Ford Media Services)

with a reinforcing plate mounted on the underside of the covers, were computer designed to minimize audible vibrations.

The shape of the engine's pistons also reduced noise. They had longer side skirts than in the past, helping to control piston movement, minimize piston slap and accompanying noise. The three-valve design also helped to reduce operating noise, as engineers were able to balance the forces generated by valve and spring movement against each other and aim the resultant force vectors toward the engine's overall center of gravity. This reduced total engine vibration and noise.

The smaller surface area of the cylinder heads helped lower radiated noise. The roller-finger camshaft followers used in the cylinder heads were more efficient and quieter than the older non-roller design. Refinements in the engine's front cover were responsible for a one-decibel reduction in overall sound levels.

Corresponding with these developments was engineering that provided the F-150 with the "right kinds" of sound. One example was the need for appropriate audible feedback when the driver stepped hard on the accelerator. Ford explained this "sound of power - only present during brisk acceleration - is created by tailoring the engine's NVH package to allow the right amount of fourth-order resonance to reach the passenger compartment. This tonal quality represents the sound of V-8 performance and is tuned through precise shaping of the intake and exhaust systems, as part of the entire HVH program."

Each Ford vehicle development team crafted its power train package to attain a specific brand characteristic. For example, while the Mustang had a 'throaty sound', the F-150 had a 'tough truck' sound under full throttle.

Matched to the 5.4 liter engine was a new 4R75E four-speed automatic transmission. Compared to the 4R70E transmission used in 2003, and again specified for the 4.6 liter V-8 in 2004, it was upgraded to handle the torque of the 5.4 liter engine. A redesigned torque converter enhanced launch

This DVD player was optional for the 2004 F-150 Lariat. (Courtesy of Ford Media Services)

120

A view of the final assembly line at Ford's Ontario Truck Plant. The last truck built at this 39-year old plant was a White 2004 Heritage F-150. Ontario Truck had been the only plant in North America to build the SVT F-150 Lightning and the 2000 Harley-Davidson F-150. (Courtesy of Ford Media Services)

performance. A turbine speed sensor was the basis of the transmission's fully electronic 'Smart' shifting schedule which limited 'hunting' between gears and fine-tuned shift speed and feel. By anticipating the torque output in the next gear, it determined the shift point based on the truck's projected performance in the next gear. A sealed case and lifetime transmission fluid made the transmission maintenance free. An adaptive pressure control maintained shift feel over time.

The use of improved gaskets, seals and crankcase-ventilation plumbing reduced the 4.6 liter V-8's hydrocarbon emissions.

The engine's new electronic fuel injection system was a returnless design with fewer components. It generated less gasoline vapor and its fuel economy was slightly improved. The injectors and a stainless-steel damper-less fuel rail produced less noise.

Both engines were subjected to testing that was the equivalent of over five million miles of normal use. They shared a new torque-based electronic throttle control (ETC) using driver input from the accelerator to actively modulate the torque at the drive wheels. In this system, a direct descendant of technology used on military aircraft, the familiar mechanical throttle linkage was replaced by an accelerator position sensor, an electronic control circuit, and an actuator at the throttle valve on the engine. The controller, after analyzing the engine's current operating status and ambient conditions, managed the throttle as required to deliver the appropriate result. This system, said Ford, "produces seamless and consistent engine response, improved fuel economy and enhanced integration of engine systems, such as transmission, variable camshaft timing, vehicle speed control, and idle speed control".

An example of the system's advantage over mechanical counterparts was its ability to tune throttle response relative to the truck's speed. For example, when starting from a stop the 'tip-in' of the accelerator was progressive and predictable, so the driver can pull away smoothly. While under way, the truck responded instantly and strongly to more pressure on the pedal.

With the stiff metal cable between a traditional accelerator pedal and the engine eliminated, so was a traditional pathway into the cab for noise and vibration. At the same time, pedal feel was less susceptible to degradation over time due to friction and wear. Ford engineers used the inherent flexibility of the ETC system to give 4x4 models a specific throttle calibration while in low range. This feature was exclusive to the F-150 and the Range Rover.

ETC also included many safety features including multiple fail-safe mechanisms for both the software and hardware redundant sensors as well as self-diagnostic software. The system was also 'fault-tolerant'. If only a minor fault is detected, 'limp-home' modes allowed the truck to move under its own power. In the case of what Ford called "the remote chance of failure", the power train control module was designed to shut the fuel injectors, preventing engine runaway.

Ford dealers still had a supply of 1965 F-100 pickups such as this attractive example when the Ontario Truck Plant began producing the 1966 models on August 26, 1965. Over the course of nearly four decades, the plant's output of light, medium, and heavy-duty trucks exceeded four million units. (Courtesy of Ford Media Services)

A close view of the front fender identification of the 2004 F-150 XLT powered by the standard 4.6 liter Triton V-8. (Courtesy of Ford Media Services)

The 2004 XLT had a standard body-color grille surround and a black honeycomb insert. (Courtesy of Ford Media Services)

122

The first 2004 F-150 Pickup completed at Ford's Norfolk, Virginia Assembly Plant on June 10, 2003 was equipped with Ford's 100 millionth V-8. With Ford's 100th anniversary less than a week away, Roman Krygier, Ford group vice president, Global Manufacturing and Quality, commented that "it is quite fitting that this milestone engine is placed in the very first 2004 Ford F-150".

At the start of the 2004 calendar year, nearly 29 million F-series trucks had been sold, making it the most successful vehicle nameplate in the world. Added to this endorsement, the most impressive ever received by a pickup truck producer, were numerous awards given to the new F-150 by a wide range of publications and organizations:

2004 North American Truck of the Year.

2004 Truck of the Year: *Motor Trend Magazine*.

2004 *Detroit News* Truck of the Year.

The Year's Best Pickup: *USA Today*.

2004 Truck of Texas: Texas Auto Writer's Association.

Truckin' Magazine Truck of the Year.

Popular Science 2003 Best of What's New Grand Award.

Top Pick of 2004 Trucks: *AMI Auto World Magazine*.

Money Magazine Best New Truck for 2004.

Kelley Blue Book Best Redesigned Vehicle for 2004.

American Woman Road & Travel Top 10 Award - Pickup Truck, Most Athletic.

FAMA Magazine Truck of the Year.

Major specifications of the 2004 F-150

Powertrain		
Engine	4.6 liter Triton V-8	5.4 liter Triton V-8
Bore x Stroke (in)	3.55 x 3.54	3.55 x 4.17
Displacement	281cu in (4606cc)	330cu in (5409cc)
Comp. Ratio	9.3:1	9.8:1
Fuel Injection	Electronic seq, multi-port	
Valve train	SOHC, 2 valves per cyl.	SOHC, 3 valves per cyl.
Horsepower	231@4750rpm	300@5000rpm
Torque	293lb/ft@3500rpm	365lb/ft@3750rpm
Oil Capacity	6qt	6qt
Coolant Capacity	20.1qt	21.1qt
Transmission	4-speed auto, overdrive,	4-speed auto, overdrive
Transmission Type	4R70W	4R70W

Gear Ratios

1st	2.84:1	2.84:1
2nd	1.55:1	1.55:1
3rd	1.00:1	1.00:1
4th	0.70:1	0.70:1
Available axle ratios	3.31:1/3.55:1/3.73:1/4.10:1	

All but the 3.31 were available with the optional limited slip differential.

Suspension

Front Coil-on-shock, long-spindle double wishbone independent, cast aluminum lower control arm.

Rear Hotchkiss-type non-independent live, leaf springs, and outboard shock absorbers.

Steering

Type	Power, rack-and-pinion
Overall Ratio	20.1:1 (short wheelbase), 17.0:1 (long wheelbase)

Brakes

Front	13.0in vented disc
Rear	13.7in vented disc

Wheels and Tires

Base tire and wheel	17in steel, P235/70R17
Largest tires available	P265/60R18 OWL All-Season with 4x2
	P275/65R18 OWL All-Terrain with 4x4
	LT245/70R with 8200 Payload Group

Dimensions (in)

	Styleside 5ft 132.5wb		*Styleside 5ft 138.5wb*	
	4x2	4x4	4x2	4x4
Overall Length	218.0	218.0	224.0	224.0
Overall Height	73.1	75.3	73.1	75.3
Overall Width	78.9	78.9	78.9	78.9
Front Track	67.0	67.0	67.0	67.0
Rear Track	67.0	67.0	67.0	67.0
Cargo Box Length	67.0	67.0	67.0	67.0
Box Width	50.0	50.0	50.0	50.0
Inside Box Height	22.3	22.3	22.3	22.3

	Styleside 6ft 125.8wb		*Styleside 6ft 144.4wb*	
	4x2	4x4	4x2	4x4
Overall Length	211.5	211.5	229.8	229.8
Overall Height	72.8	74.8	73.1	75.3
Overall Width	78.9	78.9	78.9	78.9
Front Track	67.0	67.0	67.0	67.0

continued over

Auto Journalist's Association of Canada (AJAC) Best New Pickup Award for 2004.

Top Ten Tow Vehicles: *Go Boating Magazine.*

2004 People's Choice Truck of the year.

Truck Interior of the Year: Auto Interior Show.

Truck of the Decade: Automotive/ Aerospace Industry Website.

Among the most important recognitions received by the 2004 F-150 Regular Car, SuperCab and SuperCrew models came from the National Highway Traffic Safety Administration (NHTSA) which accorded them a five-star rating in the Federal government's frontal impact crash tests. The F-150 was the only 2004 pickup to receive five-star ratings for both the driver and right front passenger. The director of the NHTSA Automotive Safety Office, Jim Vondale, commented on this achievement: "The five star ratings confirm our own analysis of the safety performance of this excellent vehicle. The F-150 has a strong record for real world safety".

Paralleling this achievement was the announcement by the Insurance Institute for Highway Safety that the F-150 had been credited with its highest ranking of "Best Pick" for the occupant protection it demonstrated in the Institute's high-speed frontal offset crash test.

These honors reflected favorably on the F-150's heritage as the world's most popular pickup and Ford's awareness of what its customers wanted in their trucks. Since the introduction of the F-1 in 1948, Ford had what Matt DeMars, Ford's

	4x2	4x4	4x2	4x4
Rear Track	67.0	67.9	67.0	67.0
Cargo Box Length	78.8	78.8	78.8	78.8
Box Width	50.0	50.0	50.0	50.0
Inside Box Height	22.3	22.3	22.3	22.3

| | *Flareside 6ft 125.8wb* || *Flareside 6ft 144.4wb* ||
	4x2	4x4	4x2	4x4
Overall Length	211.5	211.5	229.8	229.8
Overall Height	72.8	74.8	73.1	75.3
Overall Width	78.9	78.9	78.9	78.9
Front Track	67.0	67.0	67.0	67.0
Rear Track	67.0	67.9	67.0	67.0
Cargo Box Length	78.8	78.8	78.8	78.8
Box Width	50.0	50.0	50.0	50.0
Inside Box Height	22.3	22.3	22.3	22.3

| | *Styleside 8ft 144.5wb* || *Styleside 8ft 163.0wb* ||
	4x2	4x4	4x2	4x4
Overall Length	211.5	211.5	229.8	229.8
Overall Height	72.9	74.9	73.1	75.3
Overall Width	78.9	78.9	78.9	78.9
Front Track	67.0	67.0	67.0	67.0
Rear Track	67.0	67.9	67.0	67.0
Cargo Box Length	78.8	78.8	78.8	78.8
Box Width	50.0	50.0	50.0	50.0
Inside Box Height	22.3	22.3	22.3	22.3

Prices and Options

Model	MSRP
Styleside XL	
2WD Reg. Cab 6.5ft box	$21,215
2WD Reg. Cab 8ft box	$21,515
4WD Reg. Cab 6.5ft box	$24,555
4WD Reg. Cab 8ft box	$24,855
2WD SuperCab ext. cab 6.5ft box	$24,165
4WD SuperCab ext. cab 6.5ft box	$26,980
4WD SuperCab ext. cab 8.0ft box	$27,280
STX Styleside	
2WD Reg. Cab 6.5ft box	$21,865
4WD Reg. Cab 6.5ft box	$25,205
2WD SuperCab ext. cab 5.5ft box	$24,215
2WD SuperCab ext. cab 6.5ft box	$24,515
4WD SuperCab ext.cab 5.5ft box	$27,330
4WD SuperCab ext. cab 6.5ft box	$27,360
XLT Styleside	
2WD Reg. cab 6.5ft box	$24,175
2WD Reg.cab 8ft box	$24,475
4WD Reg. cab 6.5ft box	$27,590
4WD Reg. cab 8ft box	$27,890
2WD SuperCab ext. cab 5.5ft box	$26,720
2WD SuperCab ext. cab. 6.5ft box	$27,020
2WD SuperCab ext. cab 8ft box	$27,320
4WD SuperCab ext. cab 5.5ft box	$29,785
4WD SuperCab ext. cab 6.5ft box	$30,085
4WD SuperCab ext. cab 8ft box	$30,385
2WD SuperCrew crew cab 5.5ft box	$29,020
4WD SuperCrew crew cab 5.5ft box	$32,235

continued next page

XLT Flareside
2WD reg. cab 6.5ft box	$25,020
4WD reg. cab 6.5ft box	$28,435
2WD SuperCab ext. cab 6.5ft box	$27,865
4WD SuperCab ext. cab 6.5ft box	$30,930

FX4 Styleside
4WD reg. cab 6.5ft box	$29,690
4WD SuperCab ext. cab 5.5ft box	$31,885
4WD SuperCab ext. cab 6.5ft box	$32,185
4WD SuperCrew crew cab 5.5ft box	$34.185

FX4 Flareside
4WD reg. cab 6.5ft box	$30,535
4WD SuperCab ext. cab 6.5ft box	$33,030

STX Flareside
2WD Reg Cab 6.5ft box	$22,710
4WD Reg. Cab 6.5ft box	$26,050
2WD SuperCab ext. cab 6.5ft box	$25,360
4WD SuperCab ext. cab 6.5ft box	$28,475

Lariat Styleside
2WD SuperCab ext. cab 5.5ft box	$29,450
2WD SuperCab ext. cab 6.5ft box	$29,750
4WD SuperCab ext. cab 5.5ft box	$32,745
4WDS SuperCab ext. cab 6.5ft box	$33,045
2WD SuperCrew crew cab 5.5ft box	$32,115
4WD SuperCrew crew cab 5.5ft box	$35, 570

*Destination cost was an additional $795

Executive Director for Trucks, called "a long and storied history of leadership with F-series. We have a huge owner body and reputation for toughness and durability that is unsurpassed in the industry. Our well-developed customer insight helps us anticipate 'the next big thing' in the market and we continue to give customers the most appealing products like SuperCrew, like the F-150 King Ranch, the F-150 Harley Davidson, and the F-150 Lightning."

During the 1990s, Ford conducted extensive market research to gain a better understanding of consumer wants and needs. After the company polled more than 10,000 car and truck owners of various makes and models, it had a large pool of information about how these vehicles were used on a daily basis. Among the significant insights was the dramatic evolution of the full-size pick-up market. Buyers of these trucks continued to value the pickup's traditional virtues such as "workhorse" capability and functionality. At the same time customers indicated increased interest in trucks that expressed their individuality. The result was that models with more space, more versatility, more comfort, and more features grew in popularity as the pickup began to appeal to a much broader range of customers, while retaining its traditional owner base. New four-door cabs attracted more customers who were attracted to their versatility. Ford responded to the growing personal-use trend among pickup truck buyers with the SuperCab and SuperCrew variants of the F-150 that brought F-series capability to a more diverse customer base, providing product flexibility and greater choice, without compromising Ford's work truck heritage. Extended cab models started the 1990s with less than 20 per cent of the total market. By 2004, they represented approximately 80 per cent of all pickup truck sales.

As the latest F-150 debuted, the Ford F-series had been the best-selling truck in America for 26 years and the best selling vehicle in the US

The standard engine for the 2004 F-150 FX4 was the 5.4 liter Triton V-8. The FX4 had a body-color grille surround with a black-bar insert. The Dark Shadow Grey front and rear step bumpers were used on trucks with two-tone paint. (Courtesy of Ford Media Services)

An x-ray view of a 2004 F-150 SuperCrew displaying its 5.4 liter Triton V-8 engine, suspension and braking systems. (Courtesy of Ford Media Services)

This 2004 F-150 STX was equipped with the optional AM/FM radio with 6-disc in-dash CD changer. (Courtesy of Ford Media Services)

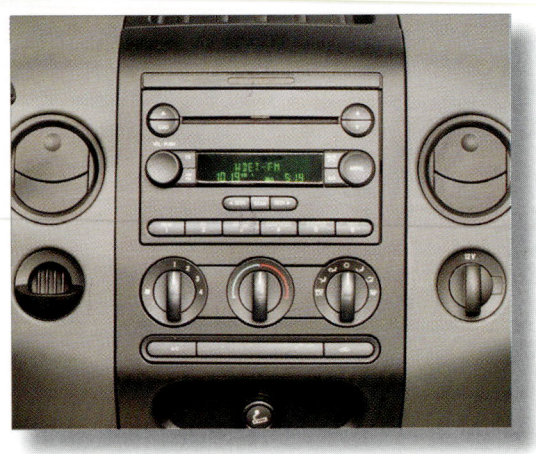

A 2004 F-150 STX SuperCab. The grille surround was painted in body color and a black bar-style insert was used. (Courtesy of Ford Media Services)

The 2004 F-150 XL was fitted with chrome front and rear step bumpers. The grille surround was also chrome. (Courtesy of Ford Media Services)

A 2004 F-150 FX4 in company with a 1955 F-100 'under restoration'. (Courtesy of Ford Media Services)

for 21 years. Fueling this success was the doubling of the market for full-sized pickups in the US within the past decade. By 2003, more than one vehicle in ten sold in the US was a full-sized pickup and three of the top ten selling vehicles in the US were full-size pickups. In major regional truck markets, full-size pickups represented 24 per cent of all vehicle sales.

Just out of the limelight surrounding the new 2004 F-150 were the F-150 Heritage models that were sold alongside the new models. The Heritage F-150s were selected versions of the models originally introduced in 1997.

Heritage models were available in XL and XLT trim in Regular Cab and SuperCab versions. Both were available with 6.5ft or 8ft Styleside boxes. Regular Cab models could be matched with a 6.5ft flare-fender box. Both 2x2 and 4x4 drive trains were offered.

The SVT Lightning model, with its 5.4 liter supercharged V-8 and sport suspension, was based on the Heritage F-150. A new Silver Metallic exterior color was offered. The only options were a tonneau cover and a bedliner.

On February 2, 2004 DaimlerChrysler's new Dodge Ram SRT-10 pickup, driven by Brendan Gaugham, a six-time winner with a Dodge Ram in the 2003 NASCAR Craftsman Truck Series, wrested the title of "World's Fastest Production Pickup" away from the SVT Light with a two-way average speed through the flying kilometer of 154.587mph.

Fully aware that DaimlerChrysler was planning a production model Dodge pickup powered by a 500 hp, 505 cubic inch Viper V-10 (the SRT was introduced on November 19, 2003), Ford had its future intentions for a new far-more powerful Lighting ready for exhibition immediately after the 2004 F-150 debuted at the 2003 North American International Motor Show in January, 2003. Depicted by its Media Service as Ford's bold vision for a third-generation SVT F-150 Lightning, neither Tom Scarpello nor John Coletti minced words when it came to talking about this truck, the first concept vehicle in SVT's ten-year history and what it meant for the SVT Lightning's future. Obviously, having the Dodge Ram SRT-10 in mind, Coletti said, "It will be nice to finally have a little cross-town rivalry,

Exclusive to the 2004 F-150 Lariat was its brushed nickel honeycomb grille insert. This 4x4 has the optional Arizona Beige two-tone paint. (Courtesy of Ford Media Services)

A 2004 F-150 Lariat 4x4 SuperCrew. (Courtesy of Ford Media Services)

but we have no intention of being overshadowed on our home turf. The SVT Lightning Concept showcases technology we're developing to meet the competition head-on."

Added Tom Scarpello, "We are excited about the new F-150 because it will provide an outstanding platform for the next-generation Lightning. The SVT F-150 Lightning concept hints at what we could do with Lightning and sends a signal that we don't intend to give up our dominance of the sport truck market."

Powering the Lighting concept was an all-aluminum, 5.4 liter dual overhead cam (DOHC), 32-valve supercharged (a Lysholm screw-type supercharger was used) and intercooled V-8. Its output, said Ford was "conservatively rated at 500 horsepower and 500 foot pounds of torque". Obliquely suggesting that when this "concept" became "production" it might have a "secret weapon" specifically intended to regain the right to be called the world's fastest pickup, Ford noted that Coletti's team had "invented and patented a speed secret for those times when even that much power just isn't enough". What was described as "Ford's patented Supercooler technology", used the truck's air conditioning system to chill a small tank of coolant to about 30 degrees Fahrenheit. As in the past, the intercooler in normal operation dissipated heat from the supercharger air by circulating coolant through a front-mounted air-cooled radiator. On demand, the SuperCooler system switched the intercooler flow from this circulation and dumped the chilled coolant into the engine's intercooler, allowing it to dissipate up to 20 per cent more heat from the charge, thus increasing its density. A green light on the instrument panel alerted the driver to the system's readiness and when the driver depressed the accelerator to a wide-open-throttle position, the system was automatically activated. As a result, as much as 50 'transient

Right: The 2004's Lightning's side-exit exhaust and 18in wheels were easy on the eye. (Courtesy of SVT Media Services)

Left and below: Two views of a 2004 F-150 4x4 XLT SuperCrew. (Courtesy of Ford Media Services)

horsepower' was available for short bursts of 30-45 seconds, the system regenerated in less than two minutes under normal driving conditions. The SuperCooler provided an effect similar to the aftermarket nitrous oxide systems, but it was completely self-contained, regenerative, and environmentally friendly.

"This technology plays directly into the hands of the enthusiast", said Coletti. "The SuperCooler provides the edge for the driver and it is done simply by taking advantage of the hardware that already exists in the vehicle."

Other aspects of the Lightning concept engine included Manley connecting rods, two fuel injectors per cylinder, and high-performance cylinder heads similar to those used on the limited edition 2000 Ford SVT Mustang Cobra R. The combination of free-flowing headers and dual side pipes produced what Ford described as "a classic American V-8 rumble".

The engine was topped by a Performance Red air intake. Both the engine and the supercharger were completely chromed and polished. The valve covers carried "Powered by Ford" lettering. A 6-speed Tremec T-56 transmission, the same as used for the 2003 Ford SVT Mustang Cobra, along with a short-throw, console-mounted shifter was installed. Ford said this shifter was "more like that of a sports car than a traditional pickup's long-shaft floor-mounted shift lever".

The concept was fitted with an independent rear suspension adapted

A 2004 F-150 FX4. (Courtesy of Ford Media Services)

Three of the 2004 SVT Lightning's most distinctive features - crystaline headlamps, clear turn signals and round fog lights are seen in this perspective. (Courtesy of SVT Media Services)

The Lightning's Silver metallic finish was new for 2004. (Courtesy of SVT Media Services)

from the current Ford Expedition. "The new architecture of the F-150 made it easier for us to adapt the independent rear suspension", said Jeff Feit, SVT Lightning chassis and powerplant engineer. "This allowed us to reduce unsprung weight even further and fine-tune the handling in true SVT style."

The front suspension was derived from the 2004 F-150 with upper control arms modified to accommodate 22in cast aluminum, six-spoke wheels and Goodyear P295/40R22 tires. P325/45R22 tires were used at the rear. Brembo disc brakes with 380mm, cross-drilled ventilated discs were used at all four wheels. The front brakes had six calipers; those at the rear had four. The 2004 F-150's new rack-and-pinion steering was also used.

The new F-150's modular design architecture made it possible for SVT to display the Lightning concept as a "possible derivative" of the F-150 at the same time it was making its debut. "Modular design", said Craig Metros, F-150 chief designer, "lends itself to special editions like this. Changing details such as the front grille, the side body panels and interior trim transforms the truck. The result is a specialized, high-performance model, far from being just a wheel-and-tire package."

The Lightning concept was based on the 2004 Regular Cab F-150 Flareside model, but in keeping with Lightning tradition, it had only two doors. This was accomplished by replacing the Regular Cab F-150's rear access doors with longer front doors and fixed B-pillars. Additional Lightning styling cues included electroluminescent gauges, side exhausts, clear taillights, and round fog lights.

The Lightning concept's exterior was dominated by its 22in tires mounted on the Gunmetal Gray alloy wheels. Crafted by F-150 designer Michael Trump, they had a sculpted, flush face and a positive off-set. The combination of a slightly chopped roof line and sharply defined panels connecting the front and rear bumpers gave the truck a purposeful profile.

Philip R. Martens, president, Ford Blue Oval Vehicles Programs and Processes presented the SVT Lightning Concept to the media at the North American International Auto Show in Detroit on January 3, 2003. (Courtesy of SVT Media Services)

Dual exhausts were integrated into the panels on both sides of the body.

The 6.5ft Flareside box had smooth stepsides, a hard tonneau cover, and an aerodynamic spoiler mounted on the tailgate's top. Twin venturi tunnels wrapped around the rear bumper. They were designed to increase stability at high speeds by reducing turbulence and generating rear down force. The concept's taillights, mounted above the bumper, had a three element design and a complex reflector under a clear lens. Unlike the production F-150, the grille of the concept was separate from the hood, creating a continuous arch from headlight to headlight. The lower fascia incorporated the SVT's cachet round fog lamps. The hood included functional air induction vents.

F-150 design manager Jim Smithbauer described the highlights of the concept's interior: "The luxurious Lariat interior was a perfect starting point for the SVT Lightning concept. The color and trim emphasizes the SVT Lightning concept's aggressive character while the seat bolsters and console-mounted shifter make the perfect cockpit for the performance enthusiast. The dash and center flow-through console are accented with Liquid Silver Metallic to match the exterior. The seats are covered in Mustard Yellow leather complemented by Ebony carpet and door trim. Even subtle changes emphasize performance, like the red engine start button and the electroluminescent gauges - an SVT trademark."

After noting that the current SVT Lightning accelerated from 0-60mph in a "scorching 5.8 seconds", Ford added a final hint of what awaited SVT Lightning enthusiasts in the near future: "the Ford SVT Lightning ... hints that the next generation Lightning will raise the bar even further and continue to dominate the sport truck arena".

The 2004 SVT Lightning continued to be powered by the 380hp 5.4 liter supercharged intercooled Triton V-8. (Courtesy of SVT Media Services)

In early January 2004, shortly after the F-150 had received the 2004 North American Truck of the Year Award at the North American International Auto Show in Detroit, Ford announced plans to expand the F-150 lineup with the addition of the 2005 Ford King Ranch F-150 SuperCrew. Perhaps because of its absence from the 2004 F-150 lineup, Ford Division president, Steve Lyons, emphasized the importance of the King Ranch and the F-150 in their

132

The appearance of the F-150 Lightning SVT Concept differed dramatically from that of the 2004 SVT Lightning. (Courtesy of SVT Media Services)

respective fields: "The King Ranch is to America's ranching industry and the western lifestyle what Ford is to pickup truck buyers. It is the perfect name to link with our new F-150 pickup."

The King Ranch F-150 SuperCrew had a 5.5ft box and was powered by the 5.4 liter 3-valve Triton V8. 18in aluminum wheels, a flow-through center console with a floor-mounted shifter, and Castano leather trim were standard.

Just over the horizon was a far more powerful V-8, code-named the 'Hurricane' and likely to displace at least 6.2 liters. Like the Triton V-8, it would meet stringent emission regulations while giving many F-150 owners what they covet most, the right to own not only the most popular pickup on the planet, but also the most powerful.

For 2005 a 4.2 liter V-6 engine with the following specifications was introduced:

Engine Type	V-6, iron block, iron cylinder heads
Bore x Stroke	3.81in x 3.74in
Displacement	256cu in (4196cc)
Comp. Ratio	9.2:1
Fuel Injection	Sequential multi-port electronic
Valve train	SOHC, 2 valves per cylinder
Horsepower	202@3750rpm
Torque	260lb/ft@4350rpm
Oil Capacity	6qt
Coolant Capacity	19.7qt
Standard Transmission	5-speed manual
Ratios	
1st	3.90:1
2nd	2.25:1
3rd	1.49:1
4th	1.00:1
5th	0.80:1

Right: An evocative, partial cut-away view of a 2005 F-150 FX4. (Courtesy of Ford Media Services)

The dash panel of the 2005 King Ranch F-150. (Courtesy of Ford Media Services)

The interior of the 2005 King Ranch had a standard low-through center console with a floor-mounter shifter. (Courtesy of Ford Media Services)

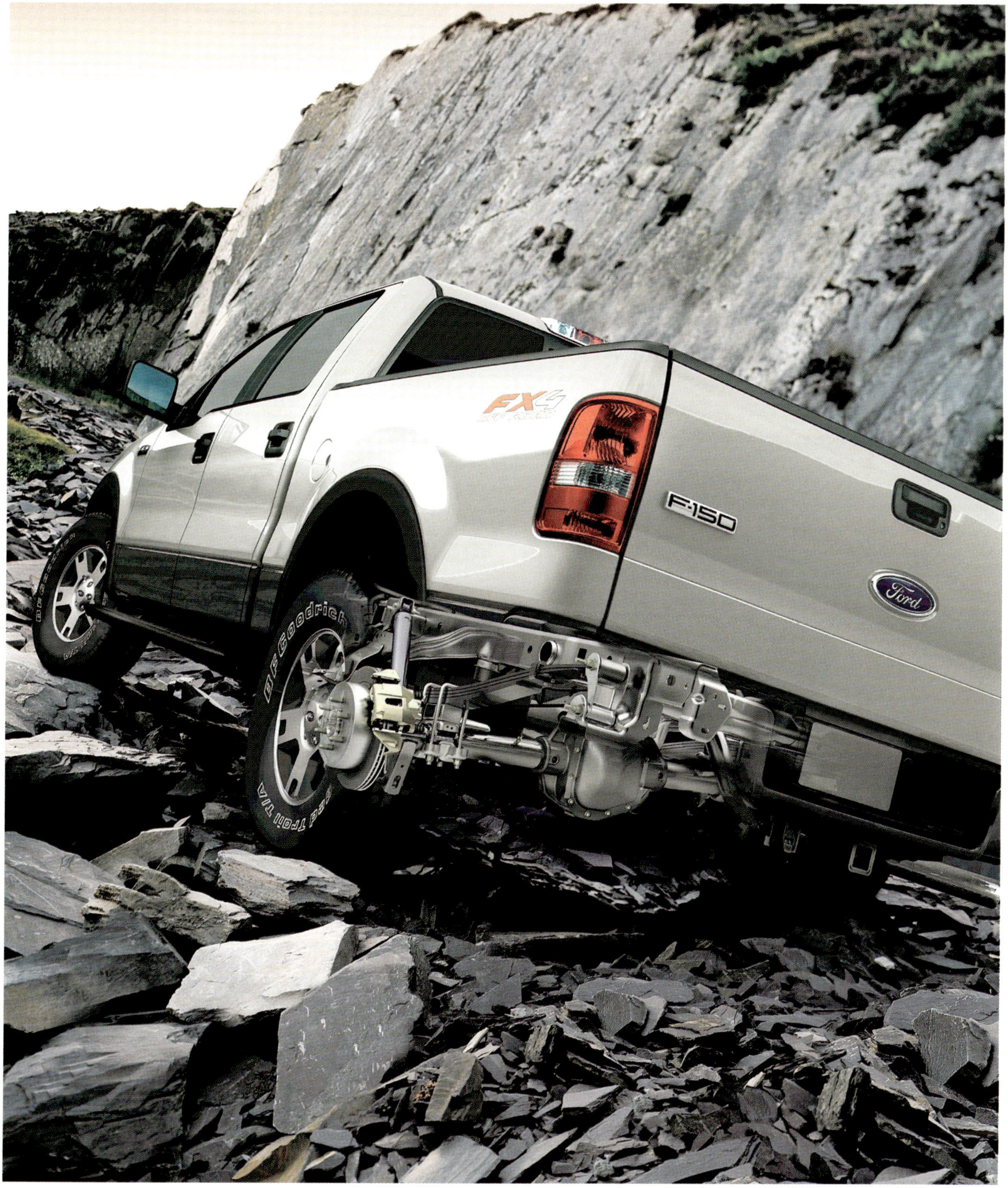
FX4
F-150
Ford
BFGoodrich

A dramatic pose by a 2005 F-150 Lariat. (Courtesy of Ford Media Services)

A head-on view of the 2005 F-150. (Courtesy of Ford Media Services)

A 2005 F-150 XL powered by the 5.4 liter Triton V-8. (Courtesy of Ford Media Services)

Also available from Veloce Publishing

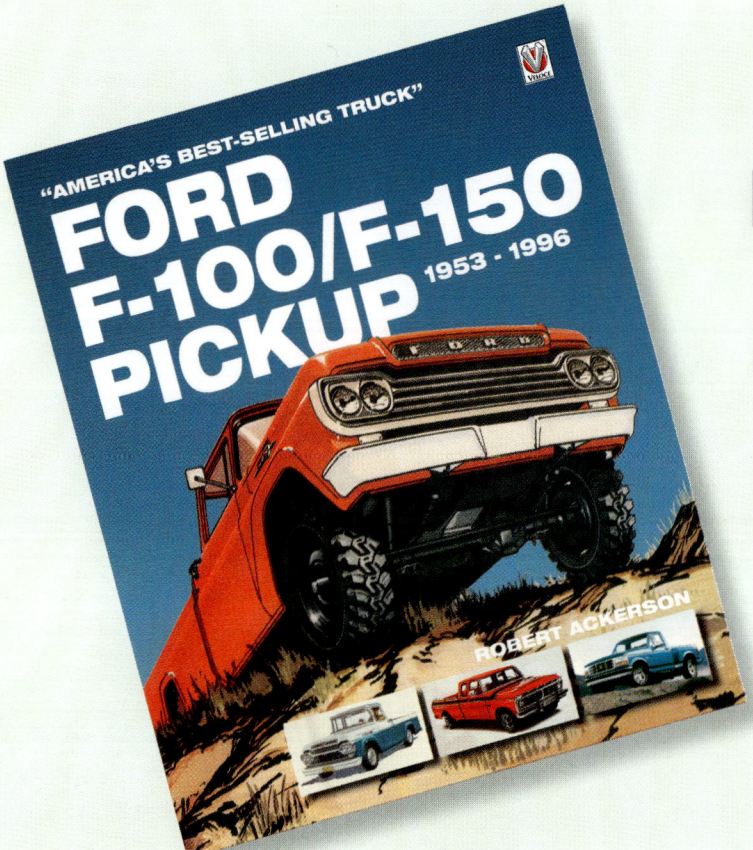

FORD F-100/F-150 PICKUP 1953 - 1996

By Robert Ackerson

160 pages, 250x207mm, 203 illustrations (40 color/163 mono), hardback.

ISBN: 1-904788-76-9

$29.95/£19.99

This book examines all aspects of the history of one of Ford Motor Company's greatest successes, its F-series pickups. Complementing a detailed text examining annual model changes, options, specifications and the unique appeal of Ford's limited edition and high-performance pickups are hundreds of illustrations, many in colour. In addition, there are chapters on restoring the first F-1 pickup of 1948 and an F-100 of 1953.

Featuring ...
- *A vivid visual display of America's most popular pickup truck.*
- *The most complete history available.*
- *Detailed specifications and photos of over 40 years of Ford pickups.*
- *A year-by-year review.*
- *Detailed information on prices and options.*
- *Examines in detail both the limited edition and mass-produced F-series pickups.*
- *An enthusiastic look at an American icon.*

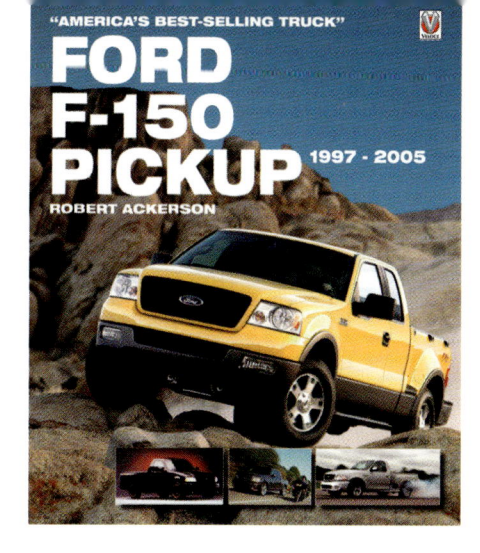

Index

Akins, Bob 7, 8
Arizona Proving Ground 11, 115

Bantam, Gerald 110, 112
Baughtman, Tom 7
Bedi, Gurminder 35, 37, 43-45
Bleustein, Jeff 37, 43-45, 60, 71
Brown, Gene 60

Captain's Chairs 9, 11, 12, 23, 31, 34, 41, 51, 60, 61, 65, 69, 71, 72, 74, 80, 81, 87, 92, 110, 111
Car and Driver magazine 30
Chapman, Tom 74
Coletti, John 62, 75, 128-130
Crew Cab 38, 90, 91

DaimlerChrysler 128
Davidson, Willie 43-45
DeMars, Matt 124
Dodge Ram SRT-10 128

Feit, Jeff 131
Flareside 7, 8, 18, 20, 22-24, 26, 30, 31, 35-37, 42, 64, 65, 76-78, 91, 107, 110, 123-125, 131, 132
Ford Expedition 51, 131
Ford Mustang 120
Ford Taurus 8
Ford, William 110, 112
France, Bill 19
FX4 model 106, 107, 110, 111, 113-115, 125, 128, 130, 135
FX4 Off Road package 66, 83, 96, 97

Gaugham, Brendan 128
Gaunt, Bobbie 38
Giombetti, Al 51, 52
Gompper, Dan 115

Harley-Davidson 35, 38, 60, 70, 71, 73
Harley-Davidson F-150 35-38, 43-46, 58, 60, 64, 69-74, 77, 86-89, 100, 101, 125

Heritage Edition F-150 72, 104, 105
Heritage F-150 128
Himes, Bob 11
Holland, Dewey 8
Hunt, Jack 61
Hurricane V-8 engine 133

King Ranch 60
King Ranch Edition F-150 58, 60, 61, 63-65, 69, 71-74, 77, 81, 98, 125, 132-134
King, Richard 60
Krygier, Roman 123

Lariat 7, 9, 11, 12, 17-20, 22-25, 30-34, 38, 41, 51, 53, 56, 58, 60-62, 64-71, 77, 79, 81-85, 91, 92, 106, 110, 111, 113, 120, 125, 129, 136
Los Angeles Times newspaper 37
Lyons, Steve 73, 107, 120, 132

Magic Air heater 16
Magro, George 36, 37
Martens, Phillip 132
Mays, J 107
Metros, Craig 131
Million Dollar Cab 16
Motor Trend magazine 12

NASCAR 19, 28, 128
NASCAR package 31
NASCAR Special Edition F-150 19, 21, 22, 24
National Highway Traffic Safety Administration 124
Nineteen-ninety Clean Air Act 24
Noltie, Brant 38

O'Connor, Jim 51, 65, 71
Off-Road Equipment Group 9, 20, 23, 25, 31, 33, 53, 62, 65

Padilla, James 107
Ptrauskas, Helen 35

139

Range Rover 121
Rouge 239 engine 16

Saturday Evening Post magazine 17
Scarpello, Tom 62, 75, 128, 129
Schiavone, Patrick 107
Scott, Doug 106
Selley, Anthony 111
Shingo Award 119
Shortridge, Charles 26, 30
Six-cylinder, 4.2 liter engine 10, 58
Six-cylinder, 4.2 liter V-6 engine 133
Six-cylinder, Essex 3.8 liter engine 10
Smithbanner, Jim 108, 132
Snow Plow Prep Group 23
Strokes, Myren 120
Sturgis Rally and Races 36, 60
STX package 19, 24, 71, 72, 102, 103, 106, 110, 112, 119, 124-126
Styleside 8, 18, 22-24, 30, 35, 36, 64, 72, 76, 77, 78, 90, 104, 107, 110, 123, 124, 128
SuperCab 7-10, 12, 14, 18, 19, 23-25, 30, 31, 35, 37, 52, 57, 58, 63-65, 67, 68, 72, 76-78, 80, 84, 85, 97, 104, 106, 107, 110-112, 115, 119, 124, 125, 128
SuperCrew 51-59, 60-66, 69-71, 73, 76-78, 80, 81, 96, 100, 110, 111, 124-126, 129, 133
SVT F-150 Lightning 26, 28, 30, 37-39, 47-49, 62, 64, 71, 74-77, 89, 105, 125, 128, 130, 131, 133
SVT Lightning Concept 129, 132, 133
SVT Mustang Cobra R 130
SVT Mustang Cobra 130

Theodore, Chris 106
Tonka concept truck 107-109
Triton 4.6 liter V-8 10, 22, 23, 31, 53, 65 , 94, 118, 122, 123
Triton 5.4 liter V-8 10, 23, 26, 28, 31, 33, 37, 56, 63, 65, 66, 70, 94, 95, 112, 116-119, 123, 125, 126, 132, 133
Trump, Michael 131

Turner, Jack 60
Twin-I-Beam front suspension 10

Volkswagen Beetle 18
Vondale, Jim 124

Ward's Auto World 53, 95, 119
Warner, Mark 112
Westphal, Bob 11
Work Series F-150 25, 30, 31, 33, 34, 37, 38, 41, 56
Work Truck option 56, 66, 80, 82

XL 7, 9, 18, 20, 22-25, 30, 31, 33, 34, 37, 38, 41, 56, 57, 64-66, 71, 76, 79, 80, 82, 106, 110, 124, 128, 136
XLT Sport Group 37, 38, 67
XLT 7, 9, 11, 12, 18-20, 22-26, 30-35, 37-39, 41-43, 51, 53, 56-58, 61, 62, 64-68, 72, 76, 79-83, 90-92, 97, 103, 104, 106, 107, 110, 111, 113, 122-125, 128, 130

www.velocebooks.com/www.veloce.co.uk
All books in print • New books • Special offers • Newsletter